Grades 5 up

People of
the Dawn

RICHARD B. LYTTLE

People of the Dawn

ILLUSTRATED BY HEIDY FOGEL

Atheneum 1980 *New York*

LIBRARY OF CONGRESS CATALOGING IN PUBLICATION DATA

Lyttle, Richard B
People of the dawn.

Bibliography: p. 171
1. Indians—Antiquities—Juvenile literature.
2. America—Antiquities—Juvenile literature.
I. Fogel, Heidy.   II. Title.
E61.L9   970.01   79-22766
ISBN 0-689-30750-0

This book is for
DON and LEE BURLESON

C O N T E N T S

Part *I* IN THE TWILIGHT

1. Ring of Stone   3
2. Beringia   13
3. "Impossible" Evidence   22

Part *II* STONE AGE AMERICA

4. Arctic Campsite   33
5. Bonanza in Stone   44
6. The Jungle's Secret   54
7. Meadowcroft   64
8. The Extinction Mystery   73
9. Happy Hunting   87

Part *III* A PLACE IN THE SUN

10. New Horizons   99
11. The Search for Corn   111
12. The City-State   120
13. The Mound Builders   132
14. Phantom Visitors   148
15. Most Civilized   158
    BIBLIOGRAPHY   171
    INDEX   174

F O R E W O R D

Although its methods have become very technical and precise, archeology is not an exact science. It never will be. Trying to reach conclusions about the past by examining a collection of relics is much like trying to reconstruct a theatrical drama from nothing more than the stage props. Archeology, in short, challenges the imagination.

Thanks to the work of hundreds of dedicated and well-trained men and women, we know a great deal about the ancient people of the New World, but huge gaps in the record and countless mysteries remain. We can deal with these gaps and mysteries only with our imaginations.

This is not a defect. On the contrary, it is a great source of fun and stimulation. No two minds work alike. Conclusions are bound to vary. Archeologists accept disagreement and conflict over their conclusions as a natural trait of their profession. And while the conclusions of the experts can guide us, we are all free to put our own imaginations to work.

It is my hope that this book will spark your imagination and lead you to your own vision of the *People of the Dawn.*

P A R T   I

In the Twilight

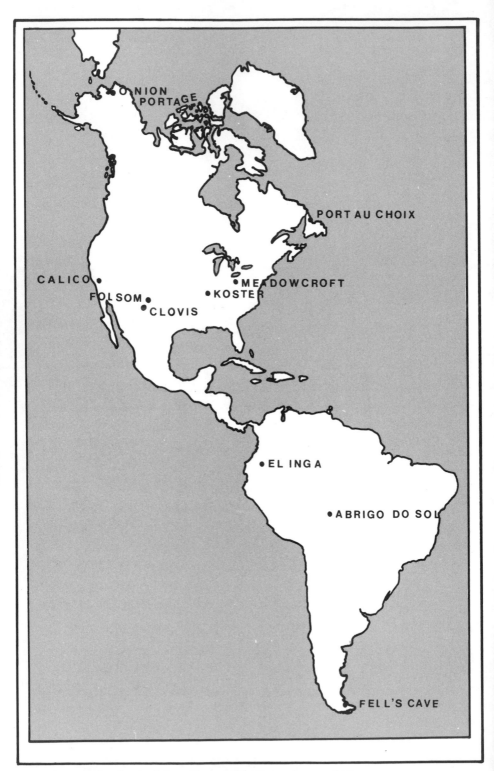

Archeological sites discussed in Parts One and Two

Chapter One

Ring of Stone

The girl scraped carefully at the caked earth. Her knife point made a soft whisper, not much louder than the sound of her own breathing. The air felt close and musty, heavy with ageless time. Indeed, at twenty-three feet below ground level, Rosemary Ritter dug in the very twilight of time.

She paused a moment to brush a pesky strand of brown hair away from her face. Then, after flexing the cramped fingers of her hand, she returned to her scraping.

Like most of the others, Rosemary had skipped classes to work at the dig. It was painstaking work, and it forced her to crouch on the dusty floor of a fifteen-foot square pit sunk in the middle of the Mojave Desert in California. Even though it was December, the days grew uncomfortably hot.

She received no pay, just a few college credits, but this didn't matter to Rosemary. For her, the possibility of discovery was all the pay she needed.

Her knife point rasped on a rock. She stopped work at once to straighten up, take off her glasses, and wipe the dust from their lenses. Then, instead of the knife, she picked up a brush before bending to the work again. She used more care than ever. She knew that the rock could be a vital clue in solving the mystery of early people in the New World.

Rocks, after all, had led archeologists to this dig. The first rocks from the site were found on the surface by an amateur collector. Ritner Sayles, a dairyman by profession, had volunteered his spare time to help the San Bernardino County Museum complete a survey of the Mojave River basin.

It was on a day back in 1948, when Sayles wandered from the river bed to investigate a horizontal line of gravel on a slope of the Calico Hills. The gravel marked the ancient shoreline of Lake Manix, a huge body of water that covered most of the desert in prehistoric times. Walking along this ancient shore, Sayles suddenly came upon several chipped rocks that seemed out of place among the water-worn pebbles.

Suspecting that the rocks might have been chipped by man, Sayles gathered them up and took them to Dr. Gerald A. Smith, executive director of the museum. Dr. Smith declared that the chips were indeed man-made, and said that Sayles had probably discovered a workshop where stone age craftsmen once made crude hand axes and scrapers.

Sayles led Dr. Smith and Ruth Dee Simpson, who was then with the Southwest Museum in Los Angeles, back to the site. The three were soon picking up other chipped stone from the old shoreline. Clearly, Sayles had discovered an important archeological site. The crude stone tools might possibly date back twenty thousand years to the time when geologists said Lake Manix began drying up.

Surface stones, however, are hard to date precisely.
Some of the experts who were asked to examine Sayles'
finds said that the chipping could have been the work of
natural forces such as landslides or flash floods, and even
though the stones appeared to be old, they might even
have been chipped recently by a rockhound or prospector.

The caution of the experts did not surprise Dr. Smith
or Dr. Simpson. Archeologists are trained to question all
evidence, but one fact was seemingly being ignored. The
stones in the collection were of good quality jasper,
chalcedony, or chert, the kind of stones that left a sharp
edge when chipped and held the edge well under use. A
concentration of such stones, chipped or not, could hardly
be credited to natural forces. Instead, it was far more likely
that they had been gathered by intelligent beings who
knew of their value as tools. Still, the evidence was ques-
tioned, and as long as questions remained, it would be
difficult to find financial backing for further work in the
Calico Hills.

Six years passed before Dr. Simpson returned to the
old shoreline and collected more chipped stones like those
Sayles had found. But the additional rocks failed to spark
interest. Another four years went by; then Dr. Simpson
made a trip to England, and fortune began to change. She
carried with her a few of the chipped stones to show to the
late Dr. Louis S.B. Leakey who, by good luck, happened to
be visiting England at the same time.

Dr. Leakey, famous for discoveries in Africa of
humanoid bones more than two million years old, had de-
voted a lifetime to his quest for traces of early man. His
opinion carried weight, and when he saw the stones from
Calico Hills, he said they had been chipped by human
hands. He promised Dr. Simpson that he would visit the
site at once, but again there was delay.

It was not until 1963, fifteen years after Sayles found the first stones, that Dr. Leakey was able to fulfill his promise. Once he arrived at the site, however, things began to happen.

He marked the spot where digging should begin, and he began organizing a staff. He would serve as project director, Dr. Smith as administrator, and Dr. Simpson as field work supervisor. Later, Dr. Thomas Clements, retired chairman of the geology department at the University of Southern California, agreed to serve as project geologist. His services would be vital because most of the dating would have to rely on geological data.

Dr. Leakey persuaded the National Geographic Society to finance the dig. The budget would be tight, but with students and amateur archeologists donating their labor, the project could begin. Dr. Leakey's name helped immensely in attracting volunteers, but one of the first volunteers needed little encouragement. Ritner Sayles was not about to miss working on the full investigation of his discovery.

The beginning was slow and discouraging. The first shaft, called Master Pit I, was started at the site Dr. Leakey had marked. Later, a second shaft, Master Pit II, was begun nearby. For several months the workers in both pits dug through layers of large rock and earth, the ancient residue of landslides. This residue, containing no evidence of early man, was ten feet thick. Below it, however, chipped stones, much like those found on the surface, began to appear.

In Master Pit II, at a depth of thirteen feet, workers found fragments of ivory from the tusk of a mastodon or mammoth. And from both pits, the collection of crude tools grew daily as the workers dug deeper and deeper, earlier and earlier into prehistoric time.

Workers at Calico were each assigned five-foot square areas in the floors of the pits.

After three years, the bottom of Master Pit II, where Rosemary Ritter worked so patiently, was on soil laid down at least fifty thousand, perhaps a hundred thousand years ago. Rosemary's steady work eventually revealed the top of an oval stone about six and a half inches long. Had it been chipped? Was it one of the primitive tools? She could have dug deeper at once to bring the rock into full view, but this was not the usual excavation procedure.

The diggers in the master pits had each been assigned a five foot square section. They were instructed to excavate their sections no more than three inches at a time. Under this system, all the earth sent to the surface for sifting by other workers could be related to a specific level, and by dropping the level of a section evenly, any relationship between two or more artifacts could be plotted with the help of a wire grid before they were removed.

It was extremely fortunate that Rosemary resisted any temptation to abandon the system because she soon uncovered the top surface of a second stone. It was close to the first one and at the same level, and as this stone came slowly into view, Rosemary could see that it was about the same size and shape as the first one.

She worked carefully around it, lowering the level evenly. It was slow work. A half hour, perhaps a full hour passed before she found yet another stone. Now, Rosemary could hardly keep her excitement in check. The three stones were in line!

When other workers came down to see the discovery, they all agreed that there was good cause for excitement.

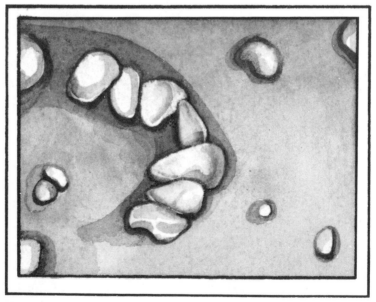

Rosemary Ritter's disovery, a hearth of stone 50,000 to 100,000 years old.

Dr. Simpson, however, told Rosemary to keep working with her same deliberate patience.

The girl nodded. Certain that she had come upon something very important, Rosemary was not about to spoil the evidence through haste or carelessness.

After hours of patient scraping and brushing Rosemary uncovered a total of nine large stones, each about six and a half inches long, and three smaller ones, about three inches long. All were linked to form an open ring or "C".

With one glance, any modern-day camper could tell immediately what these rocks represented. They formed a hearth or fireplace. Rosemary Ritter had unearthed perhaps the oldest work of human hands yet known in the New World!

Here was something to shout about, but Dr. Simpson promptly ordered that nothing be said about the discovery. Before any news of the hearth could be announced, she wanted to do everything possible to prove its authenticity and establish its age. The find would be challenged. She must be fully prepared to answer the challenge. So, as exciting as the discovery was, all at the dig agreed to remain silent.

Dr. Rainer Berger, a rock specialist at the University of California at Los Angeles, was enlisted as a consultant. He removed one of the stones from the back side of the hearth for analysis. After careful study, the rock was sliced in half. One of the halves was then sent on a long journey to a laboratory in Prague, Czechoslovakia, where special equipment could be used to determine if the rock had ever been exposed to heat.

Results were sensational. The tests showed that the side of the rock that faced into the hearth had once been heated to 752° Fahrenheit (400° centigrade). The other side had remained considerably cooler.

As a control check, several other rocks that had not been part of the hearth, but were collected from the same level were also sent to the Prague laboratory. None of them showed evidence of heating.

Meanwhile, the work on determining a firm geological date continued. The experts could not agree on an exact age for the hearth. All said it was at least fifty thousand years old, but some continued to believe that the formations at the level of the hearth could be much older, perhaps even older than a hundred thousand years.

No one rushed to any conclusions. Time, in fact, dragged. Rosemary had made her discovery in December, 1968, but the curtain of secrecy was not lifted until October, 1970. That was when Dr. Berger announced the find before the Calico International Conference, a special meeting that brought hundreds of scientists from many different nations to the San Bernardino County Museum, then at Bloomington, California.

Although many of the scientists accepted the hearth as the work of early man, the questions on its age could not be firmly answered. Geologists recognize that their dating methods cannot be exact, but some other scientists considered fifty to a hundred thousand years a loose estimate that was too broad and vague to be given much weight. As might be expected, there were some experts who declared that the chipped rocks and the ring of stones found in the Calico Hills were not the work of human hands. The ring, they said, could have been formed by some rare act of nature, and the rocks could have been heated by lightning or a forest fire.

The debate continues to this day, and Calico Hills is not the only dig that fuels the controversy over dating early occupation of the New World. At a site near Lewisville, Texas, archeologists have unearthed hearths, a stone

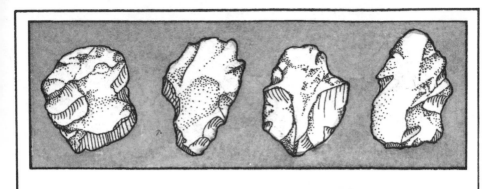

Typical artifacts of the pebble tool culture show crude workmanship.

hammer, a stone chopper, stone flakes that appear to have been left by tool makers, and the charred bones of extinct animals. Tests on charcoal found at the site show an age in excess of forty thousand years.

The same test results came from samples of bone found on Santa Rosa Island off the California coast. The bones, those of extinct pigmy mammoths, were scattered among crude stone tools at an apparent kill site. In prehistoric times, the island was connected to the mainland so it was not too surprising to find evidence of human occupation there. But the age was a surprise.

An even greater age has been given to crude tools found on the other side of the continent, at a site near Cobleskill in the state of New York. From similarity to stone tools found and dated at Old World sites, from layers of oxidation found on the stones themselves, and from the age of geological formations at the site, some experts have concluded that the tools were made seventy thousand years ago.

Collectively, all these ancient sites give support for the belief that the first Americans belonged to a pebble tool culture. They made choppers and scrapers by giving a stone, usually a river pebble, a single blow with another striking stone. Although hunters may have used wooden spears shaped to a point that was hardened in fire, they did not usually make stone projectile points, the single most useful artifacts for the identification of ancient people. And we know little else about them. We can only guess what they ate and how they fashioned their clothes. We have no idea how they buried their dead. In fact, most of the things that help define a culture are lacking.

Some archeologists even doubt that a pebble tool culture ever existed in either hemisphere. They believe that similar ages assigned New World and Old World sites present a coincidence that must be eyed with suspicion. And of course, they are the first to point out that natural forces can chip stones and charcoal and burned bones can be the work of fire caused by lightning or volcanic eruption.

Still, as more and more sites of early man are uncovered, it is remarkable that so much resistance to the evidence remains. Why is this resistance so strong and so enduring? To find the answer we must examine the Ice Age and trace the story of a land we can no longer see.

Chapter Two

Beringia

The hardest thing for European explorers to explain about the New World was its native populations. Some observers even wondered if Indians were human beings.

Early in the sixteenth century, this point was settled when Pope Julius II decreed that American Indians, in spite of their strange ways, had descended like everyone else from Adam and Eve. The Pope's decree, however, did not help solve other mysteries surrounding the Indians. Where had they come from? How had they reached the New World? When did they come? Attempts to answer these questions raised countless theories, and most of the theories were based on religious belief.

One held that the Indians descended from a lost tribe of Israel mentioned in the Bible. Another theory held that ancestors of the Indians were castaways from the Great Flood described in the Old Testament. Still another said that they descended from survivors of God's wrath at Babel. It was even stated that the devil had led these people to the New World to prevent their salvation. For a long time, some of the theories were surprisingly popular. Indeed, members of the Church of Jesus Christ of Latter-Day Saints believe even now that Indians originated in Israel. Other ancestral homes proposed for the Indians included Scandinavia, Ireland, Wales, ancient Troy, Greece, and three regions of Africa.

Vanished continents—Mu to the west and Atlantis to the east—were also envisioned as Indian homelands. The way in which the people reached these mythical places and how they had escaped their supposed destruction raised major problems, but scattered belief in Mu or Atlantis persists even to this day.

Although a few thinkers in Colonial times suggested that native Americans came from Asia simply because they looked like Asians, it was not until good maps showing the coastline of the Bering Sea were available that the true story of the world's greatest migration gradually became known. The maps show that at one point between Siberia's Chukchi Peninsula and Alaska's Seward Peninsula, the sea narrows to a strait just fifty-six miles wide. Two islands, Little Diomede and Big Diomede, stand like stepping stones near the middle of this narrow gap.

People with boats could paddle from one continent to the other and, with clear weather, never lose sight of land. For a time, while it was still thought that the New World had been recently populated, the theory was that the arrivals had all come from Asia by boat. Actually, the Eskimos, who we now know represent recent arrivals, probably did come in boats. The boat theory explaining early arrivals was, however, generally discarded in the 1930s, after several discoveries showed that humans had hunted and killed animals that had been extinct in the New World for several thousand years.

One of the most startling of these discoveries was made in Fell's Cave at the very tip of South America.

There, Junius B. Bird of the American Museum of Natural History, unearthed spear points beside the bones of sloths and horses that had died off eleven thousand years ago. Some ten thousand miles of mountains, deserts, and trackless plains lay between Fell's Cave and Bering Straits. Naturally, Bird's discovery created a sensation. It left little doubt that people had come to the New World long before boats were invented.

There was another startling thing about New World stone points and tools. Some of them, it was true, looked similar to points and tools found in Asia and other regions of the Old World, but there were others that had no resemblance to any relics yet seen. This suggested to many archeologists that the people of the New World had lived in isolation for many generations, long enough to develop their own distinct, tool-making styles and methods.

Meanwhile, biologists began making findings that complicated the puzzle. Narrow as it might be, the Bering Strait presented a barrier to the spread of most plants and animals, and yet studies of Siberia and Alaska showed that both regions supported many identical life forms. Furthermore, while some of the life found in both regions had remained unchanged for millions of years, there were other life forms, particularly mammals, that had evolved much more recently. But even these animals had occupied both the Old and the New Worlds. The biologists concluded that the two worlds had been linked by dry land for millions of years.

However, there were a few intriguing contrasts. The horse, which had originated but eventually died off in the New World, had survived in the Old World. Four different elephant species and the two-humped camel had also become extinct in the New World. Only in the Old World did elephants and camels survive. These and other subtle variations suggested to biologists that during the last hundred thousand years or so there had been periods when the land link between Siberia and Alaska did not exist. It sounded impossible, but geological study of the region showed it was true.

In some ways it is almost easier to believe the myths of Atlantis or Mu than it is to believe the scientific facts that the geologists brought to light. They found that for at least fifty million years, all through the Tertiary Period when most of today's plants and animals evolved, a continental mass joined Alaska and Siberia. This land, which we now call Beringia, was flat and dotted with many lakes and marshes. There may have been vast boggy stretches much like today's Arctic tundra. The lakes and the tundra, however, did not present a barrier to plants and animals because the land was wide, covering thirteen hundred miles from south to north, wider than the present limits of Alaska.

About a million years ago folding in the earth's crust caused a dramatic change. Beringia began to subside. The change may have happened quickly or it may have taken thousands of years. We do know that long before the emergence of modern man, the wide plain had sunk one hundred eighty feet and more below present sea level. It has not changed position since, but the sea level has changed. Changing sea levels are a phenomenon of the Ice Age.

During the height of glaciation, huge ice sheets as much as two miles thick in some places covered a third of the earth's land surface. As it advanced, the ice carved out basins that would one day become vast lakes. It crushed forests, ground rocks into sand, and changed the course of rivers. So much of the world's supply of water was entrapped in the continental ice sheets that the level of

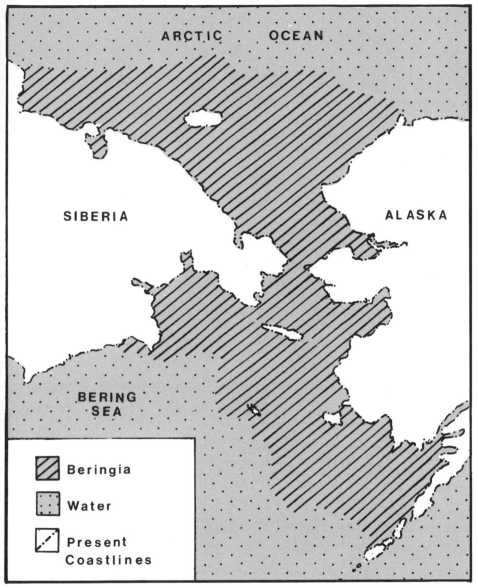

Beringia was a wide plain now covered by the shallow Bering Sea.

oceans fell by perhaps as much as four hundred fifty feet, more than enough to expose Beringia again as a dry plain.

Despite years of study, no one can be certain what caused the shift in climate that brought on the Ice Age. We cannot even say if the Ice Age is over. One theory suggests that it is not, and this theory cites the subsidence of Beringia as the cause of the climatic change.

When Beringia sank, according to the theory, warm water from the Pacific flowed into the Arctic Ocean to raise temperatures and increase evaporation there. An increase in evaporation brought an increase in snowfall on the continents bordering the Arctic Ocean. Snow, building up faster than it melted, turned to ice and the ice thickened and spread.

As the continental ice increased, the ocean levels dropped until Beringia was eventually exposed. Now warm water could no longer circulate into the Arctic Ocean. Temperatures there fell again and the sea's surface froze, bringing a decline in evaporation. Snowfall on the continents decreased sharply and the glaciers began to melt. The process thus reversed itself. Ocean levels rose. Beringia was flooded until the whole cycle was ready to begin anew. If we accept this theory, we have to say that ice sheets will once more advance across Europe and North America.

There are several other theories about the Ice Age, but the one described here is supported by the evidence of ice cycles. During the Ice Age, or the epoch that geologists have named the Pleistocene, there have been four successive advances and retreats of continental ice. The most recent advance began about sixty-five thousand years ago and lasted until thirteen thousand years ago. To the best of our knowledge, it was during this advance that modern man entered the New World.

Although the exposure of Beringia during the ice advance explained how people reached Alaska, archeologists had difficulty for a time understanding how anyone could travel southward into America while so much of it was covered with ice. For some reason, perhaps because of low precipitation, Beringia and the river valleys of Alaska remained ice free throughout the last advance, but if people tried to move inland to the higher elevations, they would have been blocked by impassable glaciers.

Although some scholars have suggested the possibility of migrations down the Pacific coast of Alaska and Canada, the route has generally been ruled out because, even with low sea level, the coastline's deep inlets and fjords probably would have blocked any travel without boats.

Again, the answer to the puzzle was provided by geologists. They found that during the last ice advance there were fluctuations with at least three major periods of thaw. The first occurred forty-five thousand years ago, the second between thirty-six thousand and thirty-two thousand years ago, and the third between twenty-eight thousand and twenty thousand years ago. A fourth and final thaw, the one that terminated the recent advance, began about thirteen thousand years ago. During each of these retreats a corridor opened in the ice sheet to provide a route to the south, probably following the Mackenzie River Valley into the Great Plains of Canada and the United States.

If the geological information stopped here, we would have a neat timetable that showed four periods when it was possible for people to cross Beringia and move into the heartland of the New World. There is, however, a complication. During the periods of thaw, water from the melting ice caused ocean levels to rise. Thus, when the corridor was opening, the route across Beringia was being flooded. We cannot be sure exactly when or how often Beringia was completely submerged. We can only say that conditions for migration were rarely ideal. It may well be that after crossing Beringia, people lived in Alaska for many generations before they were able to spread south. It is also possible that they may have been isolated, their advance blocked by ice and their retreat prevented by a flooded Beringia.

Such possibilities have turned estimating the age of New World populations into a long-running guessing game.

Back in the days before World War II, when nearly all the evidence of early man came from kill sites that were scattered with the bones of extinct mammoths or bison, it was the general belief that people did not enter the New World until the final thaw began about thirteen thousand years ago. The reasoning was that since these large animals became extinct some eight thousand to eleven thousand years ago, the kill sites had to have been at least that old. The geological evidence at the kill sites showed that they were not much older than that period. Thus, entry during the final thaw seemed to fit all available information.

After the war, however, physical science handed archeologists an important new tool for dating organic material such as bones, wood, and charcoal. All living things contain the element carbon in two different forms. One form, by far the most common, is stable, but the other form—Carbon 14—is unstable. Called an isotope, Carbon 14 has more atomic particles in its make-up than common carbon and, following the laws of physics, it can only become stable by giving up or radiating these extra particles.

Living things, absorbing both kinds of carbon through the air and through food intake, have the same proportion of stable and unstable carbon in their tissues as the proportion that occurs in nature. When the plant or animal dies and the intake of carbon stops, the proportion gradually changes as the isotope gives up its extra particles. Since this change takes place at a fixed rate, it is possible to find when the plant or animal died by measuring the proportion of the two types of carbon in its tissue. The method, far more accurate than any yet known, could determine the age of organic material that was up to forty thousand years old.

Carbon 14 dating, as might be supposed, caused a great stir among archeologists. It took much of the guesswork out of the human chronicle and it helped confirm many of the earlier estimates. It confirmed, for instance, that the big game hunting did indeed begin soon after the ice began its final retreat.

Thus, the new dating method at first supported the popular theory that the big game hunters were the first Americans, but then new evidence came to light. Carbon 14 testing of human bones found near Los Angeles gave an age of twenty-three thousand years. The bones of a child found in western Canada proved to be twenty-six thousand years old. The same age was given a hide scraper fashioned out of Caribou bone that was found in the banks of the Old Crow River in Yukon Territory.

Clearly there were migrations during the time of the second to last thaw, some twenty thousand to twenty-eight thousand years ago, when the ice-free corridor provided an entry into the New World. General agreement on the new dates had hardly been reached, however, when the finds at Santa Rosa Island, Lewisville, Cobleskill, and the Calico Hills were announced. Since the estimated age of these sites exceeded the span of the most reliable dating method yet developed, archeologists remained skeptical.

Today, most of the experts agree cautiously that people may have arrived before twenty-eight thousand years ago, but so far no satisfactory proof of such early arrivals has yet been made. This view may soon change. In fact, there is an inventive chemist in California who claims it must change.

Chapter Three

"Impossible" Evidence

The network of glass tubing, filters, beakers, and flasks looked something like the creation of a mad scientist, but Dr. Jeffrey L. Bada was perfectly sane. Obviously, he and his student assistant, Roy A. Schroeder, knew exactly what they were doing as they moved about the laboratory on the campus of the Scripps Institution of Oceanography at La Jolla, California.

They tuned gas jets, adjusted valves, and made their notes in a very efficient manner. Even the gurgling of amber liquid in the beakers filled the lab with an urgent, business-like rhythm.

The two men had a clear goal. They hoped to show that an amino acid, one of the compounds that provide the foundation for life, could be used to date bone. On this day in 1973, they were extracting a special amino acid from fragments of human bone that were thought to be very old.

The bones came from a partial skeleton that had been found some fifty years earlier in a cliff face at Del Mar, not far up the coast from the lab. M.J. Rogers, the man who found the bones, assumed that most of the skeleton had fallen into the sea. All that remained embedded in the hardened earth of the cliff was the skull, part of the jaw, and several ribs. Rogers believed the bones had great antiquity, but at the time there was no certain way to determine their age. So he wrote a detailed report and turned it and the bones over to the San Diego Museum of Man.

There the bones stayed, virtually forgotten, until Dr. Bada put out a request for samples of old bone that would serve to test his new dating method. Even when Carbon 14 testing was developed, the Del Mar bones had remained undisturbed in their museum case. There were two reasons for this. Carbon 14 testing is an expensive process, and it calls for the destruction of much of the material being tested.

Dr. Bada's method required just a small amount of material. But this was not its only advantage. The young chemist believed that his method had a much broader dating range. Carbon 14 testing could not fix a date on material older than forty thousand years. Amino acid testing, Dr. Bada claimed, might reach back as much as one hundred thousand years in time. Did he have the samples to prove such a claim? With what was known about Beringia and the ice corridor, and about the sum of evidence from New World archeological digs, it seemed extremely unlikely that the bones Rogers had found or any of the other samples sent to Dr. Bada would be much older than twenty thousand to twenty-five thousand years.

The theory behind Dr. Bada's method was simple. Amino acid molecules take two forms, one the mirror image of the other. Thus, one form will reflect light to the

right while the other reflects it to the left. In living orga-
nisms, the acid molecules all reflect light to the right, but
when the organism dies, the molecules begin to flip, be-
coming left side reflectors. Because this process, known to
chemists as racemization, occurs at a fixed rate, it should be
possible to determine the age of dead tissue simply by finding the proportion of right to left hand molecules in the
acid.

Recent development of a highly sophisticated,
$20,000 machine, called an amino acid analyzer, made it
possible to determine the proportion of the two molecules
in a matter of seconds. Using the machine, in fact, was the
easiest phase of Dr. Bada's process. Preparation of a
sample, the preliminary phase, was not so easy.

As a first step, the sample had to be cleaned with great
care to make sure that unwanted chemicals did not cause
errors. Then, because just one kind of amino acid could be
analyzed at a time, it was necessary to isolate it from all
others.

Of the several amino acids found in organic material,
Dr. Bada had chosen aspartic acid because its rate of
racemization was very slow. It could give the broad chronicle that he desired.

There was one other difficulty and it proved to be a
real problem. Although racemization occurred at a fixed
rate under stable temperatures, extreme heat or cold
would alter the rate. Dr. Bada not only had to be sure that
the sample had not been subjected to extreme temperature
changes, but he also had to estimate the average temperature on the southern California coast during prehistoric
times. He consulted many climate experts, seeking information on California and other areas of the world with
similar temperature patterns before he arrived at an
average that seemed to fit all available information. With

this figure in his equation, and with a pure sample of aspartic acid finally extracted from the bones, Dr. Bada sat down at the keyboard of the analyzer and activated its computerized circuitry.

The final phase of the process had begun. Almost at once, the rapid clack-clack-clack of the machine's printer began to type out the results. Schroeder and Dr. Bada stared at the figures. Then, they glanced questioningly at each other. It was amazing. They examined the figures again. Could it be true? Were the bones really forty-eight thousand years old?

The two men double-checked everything and ran the test again. The results were the same. They had the oldest date yet known for human remains found in the New World.

The discovery would cause a sensation, but Dr. Bada wanted to test other samples before claiming that his new method was absolutely valid. He had other samples, ten in all, and one sample would provide a significant check.

These were the bones of a Los Angeles man, which had already been given an age of twenty-three thousand years by Carbon 14 testing. The racemization method put the age at twenty-six thousand years. This was close enough to give Dr. Bada increased confidence. He turned to other bone samples from California sites.

The results continued to astound him. Although three samples were little more than thirty thousand years old, three others had ages in excess of forty-four thousand years. The bones from another skeleton found near Los Angeles proved to be fifty thousand years old. The most remarkable result, however, came from the test of human bone found near Sunnyvale, California, not far south of San Francisco Bay. According to amino acid racemization, the bone was sixty-five thousand years old.

Dr. Bada described his new dating method and published his findings in August, 1975. Of course, archeologists who had developed a case for a pebble tool culture in America found support from Dr. Bada and endorsed his new method. The majority of archeologists, however, remained cautious, saying that the method was too new to be accepted without a great deal of additional testing on many other samples.

Perhaps, if the first samples tested had not shown such remarkable ages, support for amino acid dating would have been more enthusiastic. As it is the dates are still hard to reconcile with what we know of Beringia and the ice-free corridor. The dates also run counter to what we know of the rise of modern man.

Sometimes called Cro-Magnon man, modern man is known scientifically as *Homo sapiens sapiens,* which can be translated loosely as "man who is doubly wise." Apparently originating in the Middle East, this breed was probably established throughout Asia by about forty thousand years ago, and through Europe about thirty-seven thousand years ago. Although these ages are still much debated, modern man for a time is believed to have shared the earth with another breed.

Neanderthal man *(Homo sapiens neanderthalensis)* occupied most of the Old World for at least one hundred thousand years. A successful hunter and gatherer, Neanderthal man was stockier and perhaps stronger than modern man, but with a low, sloping brow and smaller brain cavity, he was not as intelligent.

It may be that the difference in intelligence alone explains why modern men replaced Neanderthals, but the complete disappearance of Neanderthals poses some problems. Perhaps the two breeds fought with victories repeatedly going to the smarter warriors. Perhaps there was

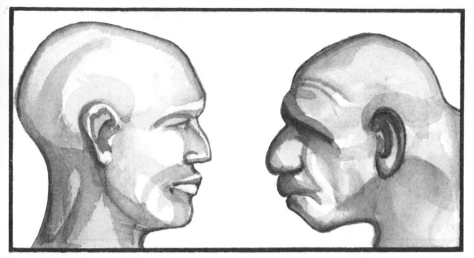

Profiles accent the difference between Neanderthal man on the right and modern man on the left.

cross-breeding with genetic domination going to modern man so that Neanderthal traits vanished. Perhaps Neanderthal man lacked immunity to some disease and was wiped out by epidemic. It has even been suggested that Neanderthals practiced unsanitary funeral rites such as delayed burial, which invited pestilence.

In Ice Age Europe, the Neanderthal people lived in caves where they made shrines of animal skulls. Thus, they are cited as the inventors of religion. They were also the first to make spear points of stone, but generally their tools were crudely chipped choppers and scrapers.

Scholars cannot agree what role Neanderthals played in the ancestry of modern man. Some say that the breed was an off-shoot of human evolution with little influence on the development of modern man, while others believe Neanderthals were an important ancestral link in human evolution. All we can say positively is that Neanderthals were replaced by modern man, and that this transition was completed about thirty thousand years ago.

Modern man prospered in a difficult environment. This furless creature, without claws and fangs, emerged when ice covered a third of the earth, and when cave bears, dire wolves, sabertooth tigers, and other hungry carnivores stalked the land.

It was a struggle for people to find enough food to stay alive. They ate anything they could find—seeds, roots, berries, insects, snakes, lizards, and rodents. At first they lacked the weapons to hunt big game such as the mammoth, horse, camel, giant bison, and other beasts. When improved hunting tools and methods did develop, success brought an increase in population that resulted in competition for hunting grounds. The people migrated in search of new territory and unwary prey.

According to most students of modern man, it was at this stage of expansion, which began no earlier than thirty thousand years ago and perhaps just twenty-five thousand years ago, that hunters had gained both the motivation and the skill to move northward into the Arctic regions of Siberia and from there into the New World.

Accepting forty thousand year-old evidence of human occupation in the New World thus forces drastic adjustment of this generally accepted theory as well as serious consideration of some startling possibilities. It might mean that the first arrivals, instead of being modern men, were Neanderthals. Most scholars find this notion very difficult to treat seriously, but the truth is that we know very little about Neanderthal man. Although he was primitive, we cannot say for certain that he lacked the ability to travel and survive in Arctic regions. Another startling notion raised by acceptance of evidence forty thousand or more years old is that modern men, for some reason, spread eastward into harsh climates of Siberia and North America far more swiftly than he spread westward into milder European territory.

Could these early arrivals have been sun worshippers? Many primitive people were, and for them the rising sun with its gift of warmth and light fulfilled their faith, renewed their hope, and promised better horizons. If there was a friendly land with warm days and nights, a land rich with game and seeds and berries, it lay to the east beyond the sunrise. These sun worshippers, moving ever eastward until they were finally drawn to the New World, might well indeed have been the people of the dawn.

Can we say what the people believed or how they worshipped? Do we know their level of culture, their degree of skill? How did they exist? What did they eat and how did they obtain their food? What did they use for shelter and clothing? What beliefs and skills did they bring with them from the Old World, and what beliefs and skills did they develop after their arrival and isolation in the New World? How did they organize their families, govern their bands and tribes? How did they discover agriculture? What led them to build temples and great cities? What powers created their empires?

Seeking the answers to these and many other questions is the real business of New World archeology. We may never know when the first arrivals began, but thanks to the careful exploration of many rich sites, the exhaustive study of relics, and the free exchange of information and ideas we know a great deal about who these people were and how they developed.

True, the picture is far from complete, and much of our knowledge is based on guesswork. But as the digs continue, we discover more every day.

Perhaps, the most striking thing that has been discovered so far is the endless variety of the New World people. While some were building roads and aqueducts in the South American Andes, others were grubbing roots and catching small game for a miserable existence in North American deserts. While some made skillfully decorated pottery, others had not yet mastered crude basket making. While some slaved in the service of priests or kings to build temples or cities, others roamed proud and free in loosely governed bands.

Yet, despite this variety, we will find in the digs and the search for clues described in the following chapters that there were threads of conformity that sometimes stretched from one end of the Americas to the other. Similarities in cultures far removed are often hard to explain, but we know that tribes borrowed skills and methods from their neighbors. We know there was trade. We know that different peoples, each having different languages and customs, were often united by a common religion.

As cultures advanced from a stone age existence to the beginnings of agriculture, and finally to the rise of civilization, these threads of conformity strengthened. Yet, we cannot generalize. Although the influence of city states eventually stretched far from their centers, the variety remained. In adapting to their distinct climates and habitats the people of the New World left unique legacies. It is the wealth of these varied legacies that remains for us to understand and appreciate.

P A R T   I I

Stone Age America

Chapter Four

Arctic Campsite

During the summer of 1940, J. Louis Giddings, Jr., an archeology student at the University of Alaska, rafted down Alaska's Kobuk River in search of ancient Eskimo settlements.

North of the Arctic Circle, the river flows westward to enter the Chukchi Sea at the head of Kotzebue Sound, which covers a small part of submerged Beringia. At one time, the valley of the Kobuk may well have been the gateway to the New World.

Today, the valley is a solemn land, sparsely dotted with willows, spruce, and birch. Not far to the north the trees give way to the tundra, which stretches beyond the horizon to the shores of the Arctic Ocean two hundred and seventy miles away.

Giddings began his journey far up the river where he built a raft and poled it into the current. Although he traveled alone, hardly a day passed when he did not meet Eskimo fishermen and their families. Sometimes, Giddings spent the nights with the Eskimos in their salmon camps. He always asked about early settlements, and the natives often were able to guide him to the ruin of an Eskimo house.

From borings taken from old timbers, Giddings was able to fix the age of the ruins with tree ring dating. Many of the ruins he examined were five hundred years old. This was not a startling age, but Giddings' summer project proved that tree ring dating, then a new method, could be used effectively in Arctic regions. And near the end of his journey, Giddings discovered Onion Portage.

All down the river, the Eskimos had been talking about Onion Portage. It was at a five-mile bend in the river, and fishermen and hunters, to save themselves five miles of hard, up-river paddling, would carry their canoes across a sandy flat. When they reached the river again, they would often camp at the base of a high knoll. Hunters sometimes climbed the knoll to watch for migrating caribou.

It was a pretty spot, with wild onions blooming along the river bank, and from the knoll, the views up and down the river were spectacular.

Giddings investigated Onion Portage and found house ruins there as old as any he had seen on the Kobuk, but the most exciting thing about the site was the apparent stratification of the soil. For ages flood water had washed silt down from the knoll, and winds had covered the site with thin layers of sand. The silt and sand lay in thick deposits.

The summer season, always short in the Arctic, came to an end before Giddings could determine how thick the deposits might be, but he knew he had to return to Onion Portage.

Stratified sites are rare in the far north where the land is either mountainous and rocky or flat and boggy. Boggy land, the tundra, shifts when it freezes, preventing any stratification, and there is not enough loose earth in the mountains for layers of soil to form. These conditions had long hampered Arctic archeologists.

A stone knife a thousand years old might be found next to one ten thousand years old, but even though the two knives might be quite different in design, there was no way to determine which was the older, which came first in the story of Arctic man. Relics found in stratified soil, however, would tell how the story unfolded.

Giddings returned to Onion Portage in the summer of 1941. He brought a friend, a fellow archeological student, and with the help of Eskimos, they began digging. The work was hampered by rain. The natives told them it was the wettest summer in their memory. The Kobuk rose over its banks. Silt and mud from the knoll flooded the camp. Careful excavation was almost impossible.

Giddings and his companion, however, did manage to excavate five old houses, and a few inches beneath the floor of one of the houses, Giddings unearthed microblades. He was astounded.

Microblades, tiny flakes about a quarter-inch wide and no longer than a needle, were made by chipping at a larger rock that had been trimmed to the proper thickness. At the time of Giddings' discovery, the only other microblades known in Alaska came from the Campus Site at the University of Alaska in Fairbanks. Other microblades had been discovered in Siberia, Mongolia, and Japan. They were believed to be very old—the oldest were from the Japanese island of Hokaido and the Kamchatka Peninsula in Russia—but in 1941, no one knew what purpose microblades had served.

Today, after the small blades have been dug from many other sites in Alaska, it is known how they were used. The blades were set into grooves carved in bone,

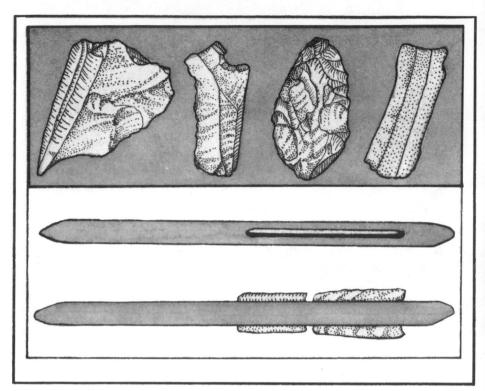

Microblades, no longer than a needle, took many different shapes (top), but all served as cutting edges when fitted into the shaft of a wood or bone weapon (bottom).

ivory, or antler spear points to give sharp, protruding edges that would cut through flesh.

As Giddings' career progressed, he became one of the authorities on microblades and the ancient people who made and used them, but in that wet summer of 1941, he was mystified by his find. If microblades were indeed old, what were they doing a few inches under the dirt floor of a house ruin little more than five hundred years old?

Giddings' only guess was that the Eskimos who built the house had found the blades at a lower level and saved them as a curiosity. The theory was thin perhaps, but Giddings had to be satisfied with it for several years.

World War II brought an end to archeological digs, and after the war, Giddings worked hard to complete his graduate studies. He did not return to the high Arctic until the summer of 1948, and then, instead of going to Onion Portage, he headed for Cape Denbigh on the coast of the Bering Sea. Almost two hundred miles south of Onion Portage, the Cape Denbigh site yielded a rich store of microblades—the biggest collection yet found in the Arctic.

Encouraged by the Cape Denbigh discovery, Giddings turned his attention to Cape Krusenstern, another beach site. This site was close to the mouth of the Kobuk River, and here again, Giddings found microblades, but he also found evidence of an amazing variety of other Arctic cultures. People who made pottery, others who carved wood, and still others who carved ivory had lived on the Kursenstern beaches. Some people existed almost entirely on caribou. Others hunted whales, and still others were seal hunters.

Remarkable as the beach finds were, however, Giddings and other Arctic archeologists were frustrated by a legacy of the ice age. When the land ice melted, the sea level rose, and the rising waters had not only covered Beringia, but had also covered all the older campsites along the beaches. It meant that nothing could be found in coastal digs that was more than three to five thousand years old. Perhaps, older evidence of man could be found up the valleys, away from the beaches. Giddings returned to Onion Portage on July 5, 1961.

Although he was often credited with an uncanny instinct that led him to rich sites, Giddings, a professor at Brown University with many summers of Arctic field work behind him, was guided more by knowledge and experience than instinct. And, of course, he had never forgotten the campsite on the big bend of the Kobuk River.

After clearing away the wild roses that had covered

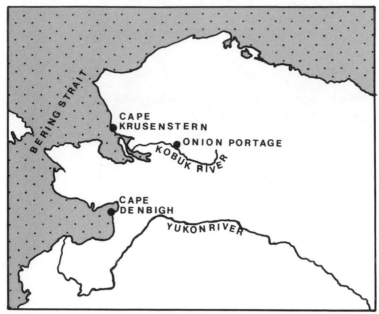

*Of the three Alaskan sites developed by J. Louis Giddings, Jr.,
Onion Portage revealed the longest record of human
occupations.*

the site of his twenty-year-old dig, Giddings began a careful probe into the first fresh layer of stratified soil. He was
rewarded at once with the discovery of black earth, a mixture of charcoal and short bits of caribou bone, typical
signs of Indians who crushed and boiled bone to make a
rich marrow soup. Soon stone and obsidian points, knives,
and scrapers came to light to confirm that Indians or
people with Indian traditions had camped at Onion Portage before the Eskimos.

The Indian-like finds proved to be about a thousand
years old, but there were still older deposits deeper down.
Giddings was eager to learn just how deep the deposits
might be, but digging was not easy. Often he and his helpers were delayed by frozen ground. Summer rains brought
discomfort and further delays.

After three summers, however, Giddings knew that he
had found a remarkable site—deeply stratified ground that
was rich in relics of early man. What would it reveal?

Tragically, Giddings could not complete the work he had begun. In 1964, at the age of 55, he died of injuries received in a traffic accident.

His three seasons of work, however, had revealed enough to assure continued exploration at Onion Portage. Froelich G. Rainey, director of the University Museum at the University of Pennsylvania, and Douglas D. Anderson, one of Giddings' former students, were invited to take over the dig. Later, Anderson was given sole direction of the work.

Now it can be said that Onion Portage not only turned back the pre-historic clock by thousands of years for Arctic man, but also solved the puzzle of other undated or poorly dated relics found before and since in the far north. The oldest relics found at Onion Portage are at least eighty-five hundred years old, and Anderson believes that some finds may prove to be as much as fifteen thousand years old, but the variety of the Onion Portage relics, the different cultures they represent, is just as significant as their age.

At a depth of twelve feet, the oldest stone tools represent a culture that Anderson has called Akmak, the Eskimo word for chert. Most of the tools at this level are made of this hard stone.

Some of the tools are biface knives and disks made by repeated flaking on both sides of a stone to give it a cutting edge. The Onion Portage disks, the first ever found in Alaska, are about five inches in diameter and could be used as choppers or scrapers. Remarkably, they match almost exactly biface disks discovered near Lake Baikal in central Siberia, at sites that are twelve thousand to fifteen thousand years old.

The Akmak people also made microblades and larger blades struck from a stone core for use as knives or scrapers. While the disks and microblades suggest close Asian ties, Anderson believes there is enough difference in Akmak tool craft to conclude that these people were isolated for a long time.

The Akmak occupation of Onion Portage, which started perhaps as early as 13,000 B.C. when Beringia was exposed, continued until 6500 B.C., well after the bridge between Asia and Alaska was covered by the rising seas. Anderson also believes that land ice prevented the Akmak culture from spreading into other regions of North America.

The Kobuk culture, which followed the Akmak, with many of the same traditions, did spread out. Anderson dates the Kobuk relics, found nine to eleven feet below the surface, at 6200 to 6000 B.C. Judging from the silt deposits, this was a wet period, and Onion Portage was apparently used only seasonally, probably as a spring and fall hunting camp during the caribou migrations.

The collection of tools—microblades, scrapers, and

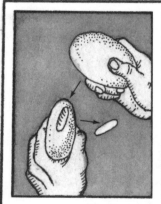

The biface disk was made by flaking off bits on both sides of a round, flat stone by hitting it with another stone.

carving tools known as burins—is small, indicating brief occupations, but similar collections have since been found at many other inland and coastal Arctic sites.

After the Kobuk culture comes an unexplained gap in the record of two thousand years, and when people occupied Onion Portage again in about 4000 B.C. they represented an entirely different tradition.

Anderson correlates this change to the warming climate that followed the ice age. This warming phase reached its peak between 4000 and 2000 B.C. and it brought a northern advance of the tree line. As forest invaded the tundra, forest-oriented cultures came to Onion Portage.

These people made large, irregularly-shaped knives, thin scrapers, and crescent or disk-shaped choppers. They also notched stones for fishnet sinkers. They did not make microblades, but instead used crude stone points on their throwing weapons, points flaked on both sides and notched at the base. Over the years, however, the style of the points changed to a stemmed base and finally a straight base.

Anderson groups these tools in the Northern Archaic Tradition, which originated in the eastern woodlands of what is now the United States and Canada. Archaic tools, found from four-and-a-half to seven-and-a-half feet below the surface at Onion Portage, match some of the oldest tools discovered by Giddings at Cape Krusenstern, a hundred and fifteen miles to the west.

The Archaic tools differ so much from those found below them, that Anderson is convinced they represent a great shift in population, not a gradual transfer of tool making styles.

After about 2300 B.C., with a return of colder weather, the Archaic Tradition was replaced by the Arctic Small Tool Tradition at Onion Portage. The Arctic tools occur from one to three-and-a-half feet below the surface, and they include burins and microblades made for insertion in the grooves of cutting tools and weapons.

The inserts, however, differ from blades made by the earliest residents of Onion Portage. Instead of being straight-edged, the microblades at this level are carefully flaked to form half-moon blades. Collections of this type have been found at many other Arctic sites, including Giddings' Cape Denbigh.

Some archeologists believe that the people of this tradition were the direct ancestors of modern Eskimos. Their tool styles, however, changed through the centuries.

From about 1500 to 500 B.C., an early Eskimo culture called Choris left relics at Onion Portage. These people made pottery, the first in Arctic regions, and their pots were so skillfully made right from the start that it seems certain the potting craft was introduced from some other area and did not evolve locally.

Choris tool collections also include large, regularly-shaped spear points very much like spear points made by hunters of the American Great Plains between 7000 and 3000 B.C. Some archeologists have suggested from this similarity in points that the Choris culture evolved from early Indians of the Great Plains, or that both cultures had a common origin. Anderson believes, however, that the age he was able to assign Choris collections at Onion Portage disproves the theory. The Choris points simply are not old enough to be linked directly with the Great Plains points.

Above the Arctic small-tool relics, broken caribou bones and Indian-like tools, give evidence of another brief change in tradition, but the people who left these relics were soon replaced by direct ancestors of Eskimos. Since 1000 A.D., the site on the big bend in the Kobuk River has been an Eskimo campground.

The story read from the strata is thus long and varied,

and it was proven to be an extremely valuable story. Relics from throughout the Arctic can now be related to a clear chronology.

Those who first camped at Onion Portage had roots in Siberia. At first, they hunted on the tundra, but later they became coastal hunters. In a treeless land, they learned to make weapons of bone, antler, and ivory with small blade inserts. With a change in climate and the northern advance of the forests, these people were replaced by forest dwellers who made their weapons of wooden shafts and stone points. Then, with the return of the tundra, Arctic traditions appeared and spread throughout the far north to establish a tool-making craft whose progress has been all but unbroken until modern times.

Today, Arctic archeologists have turned to other sites, seeking older evidence of man. At Old Crow, a site in the Canadian Yukon, diggers have found tools of stone and bone that are believed to be twenty thousand to thirty thousand years old. At Dry Creek, a site seventy-five miles north of Fairbanks, eleven-thousand-year-old relics have recently been found, and because the creek lies in a valley that remained ice free during peak glaciation, archeologists are confident that much older stone age relics will soon be discovered there.

As the collection of tools left by early dwellers in the Arctic grows, comparison with tools found in other areas of the New World will gain significance and broaden our understanding of Stone Age America. Such comparisons at other sites have already yielded tantalizing clues. Take, for example, the story of a site far off in the high Andes of South America.

Chapter Five

Bonanza in Stone

The taxi cab carrying two archeologists and a native driver labored up the twisting road. Though they were at the Equator, they had climbed so high, over nine thousand feet, that the air was cold and held the smell of melting snow.

The driver knew the route well, but the men in back kept glancing down at the map spread on the seat between them. Both men had long experience in the field, but never before had they started on an expedition in a taxi. They were amused, but also a little uneasy about the experience.

Dr. William J. Mayer-Oakes of the University of Manitoba in Canada and Robert E. Bell of the University of Oklahoma had been brought together through their specialties, the study and comparison of stone age tools. Now, after having just landed at Quito, Ecuador, they were off to investigate a site that had been discovered by an amateur archeologist.

The amateur, A. Allen Graffham, a geologist who had worked three years in Ecuador, spent the weekends with his family exploring the mountainous country around Quito in search of stone age relics. His most exciting discovery was a field littered with fragments of obsidian. From the quantity of fragments, he believed that the field must have once been the site of a virtual factory for stone tool makers.

When Graffham's geological job ended in Ecuador in 1959, he took a collection of fragments back to the United States and showed them to Bell. The archeologist was startled to see that some of the pieces appeared to be broken dart or lance points with fluted bases.

The fluting suggested a link with big game hunters who killed extinct animals on the Great Plains of North America some twelve thousand years ago. For years, South American archeologists had been unable to establish such a link. Only recently had a single fluted point been discovered in Costa Rica, but here, in Graffham's collection, from a site even farther south, were many examples of the fluting tradition.

Not all the fragments showed fluting. In fact, there was a surprising variety of workmanship and styles represented in the collection. Bell asked Mayer-Oakes to examine the fragments, and the Canadian archeologist found more cause for excitement. Some of the pieces had fishtail stems very much like the stems on points found at Fell's Cave at the very tip of South America by Junius B. Bird. For many years, the Fell's Cave points stood as the earliest evidence of human occupation in South America.

It was obvious to both Bell and Mayer-Oakes that Graffham had made an important discovery and that the site should be investigated further. Unfortunately, Graffham himself could not return to Ecuador, but he sketched a map showing how to find the site and recommended a taxi as the best transportation. He even gave the two men the name of a taxi driver in Quito who was familiar with the country.

After they arrived in Quito, Bell and Mayer-Oakes had no difficulty in locating the driver and arranging the trip. Now, on a January day in 1960, they were climbing into the mountains by cab. The site was some fifteen miles east of the city, not far from the banks of the Inga River. It was farming country, and most of the fields level enough for crops had been plowed.

The map and the bare plowed earth made it relatively easy to locate the site. Many scattered fragments of obsidian lay on surface not far from the road.

The site was spotted with small knolls or hummocks that were gradually being reduced by erosion. The erosion had exposed the obsidian.

On this first visit, the two men made a quick survey and found that the concentrations of obsidian seemed to cover some 5,000 square feet. They found no evidence of burials, no animals, no charcoal, but the site was indeed a workshop where stone age man made projectile points and other tools out of the volcanic glass that was evidently hauled from Antisana Mountain twenty-one miles to the southeast.

Time was limited for Bell and Mayer-Oakes. This season they had just two weeks to survey and collect representative samples of points and fragments, but they used their time well. Their brief work proved fruitful.

Commuting daily by taxi to the site, which they now called El Inga, they sank test pits that revealed a relatively shallow deposit. During recent times, the top ten inches of soil has been regularly disturbed by plowing. Below, however, lay eighteen to twenty inches of dark soil containing much obsidian. Under this layer, a hardpan of yellow soil yielded no relics.

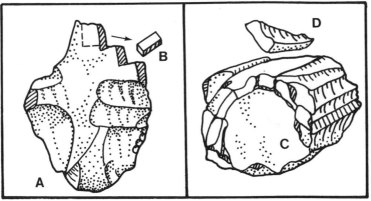

Advanced stone craft included both the making of the burin carving tool (A) by chipping away an angular spall (B), and the core (C) and flake (D) method of producing dozens of equal-length blanks for blades and points.

When time came for them to fly home, Bell and Mayer-Oakes had collected six hundred pounds of obsidian points and fragments. The collection was crated for shipment to the University of Oklahoma, where it could be studied in leisure. Before boarding their plane, they decided that at least one of them must return the following season and conduct an extensive dig. But as it worked out, their collection from two weeks of work was enough to tell a great deal about El Inga.

There were some surprises. Most of the blades, it turned out, were produced from cores. El Inga represented a core-blade industry, usually associated with sophisticated, advanced stone age people such as the Upper Paleolithic cultures in Europe, Asia, and North America. El Inga provided the first evidence that this culture was established in South America.

The core blade method requires preparation of a large stone or blank. By striking the blank at its edge a series of blades can be struck off with equal length and shape. It's something like slicing a loaf of bread, with each slice taking its shape from the shape of the loaf. The blades can be used for knives or scrapers with little additional flaking, or they can be shaped into points.

Another surprise was the discovery of burins. Again, El Inga provided the first evidence of burins in South America. A burin is an engraving or punching tool that served many uses. It could cut or punch holes in hides. It could carve lines or designs in bones or wood, and it served in carving ornaments out of shell or stone. It was the tool of an artisan.

Burins are made by chipping a small angular flake or spall from the corner of a blade to produce a sharp point. Burins and hundreds of spalls produced in making them made up much of the initial El Inga collection.

The collection also showed remarkable variety. Some of the blades were unifacial, being worked on just one side. Others were bifacial, having been chipped on both sides to produce a cutting edge. The points in the collection could be related to points discovered at several different sites throughout North and South America. El Inga, in fact, seemed to be a major tool making center, a hub of many cultures in the Western Hemisphere.

It was Bell who returned to the site in 1961 and organized a crew of local workers for three months of excavation. The crew dug a trench two hundred feet long and five feet wide through the largest of the uneroded hummocks. Later, they expanded this trench at several places. They sunk all these excavations at least two feet to reach the hardpan of yellow earth. The digging, however, was done in slow stages, with just four inches shaved away at a time. All the earth was screened, and everything found was labeled according to depth and location.

The layering of tool-bearing soils suggested an intermittent occupation for four thousand to five thousand years. The tool makers camped at the site. Unfortunately,

Bell could find no campfire residue, human burials, or any other organic material that would serve to date the finds, but from relating style and technique of the points to points found at other, dated sites, it was clear that first use of the workshop began at least ten thousand years ago, and very probably much earlier.

Bell took his collection from the 1961 excavation to Oklahoma for study, while Mayer-Oakes took the collection taken from the surface in 1960 to Manitoba. Of more than fifteen thousand pieces in the 1960 collection, Mayer-Oakes selected sixty-five hundred that were obviously tools. Among these were a wide variety of unifacial blades, gravers, scrapers, and chisels. There were some fifty burins and hundreds of burin spalls.

The bifacial tools included choppers and cleavers and grinders made of basalt, knives and scrapers made of obsidian, and of course, obsidian projectile points. There were just twenty-three unbroken points and two hundred four point fragments.

Many of the points were in what Mayer-Oakes calls the Fells Cave style, fluted or having fishtail stems. Others were leaf shaped, longer lance shaped, or shaped with long stems. He has related one or more of these shapes and styles to points found at sites in Alaska, Greenland, Canada, the Great Plains and the Atlantic Coast of North America, Mexico, Costa Rica, Venezuela, and the southern tip of Argentina. Surprisingly, the tools found at El Inga can even be matched with tools found at a stone age site in France.

This, Mayer-Oakes hastens to say, does not mean that there was some transatlantic visit to America by early French tribes. But the similarities do show that the Paleolithic culture was stable, existed for a long time, and was wide spread. During the thirty-five thousand and more

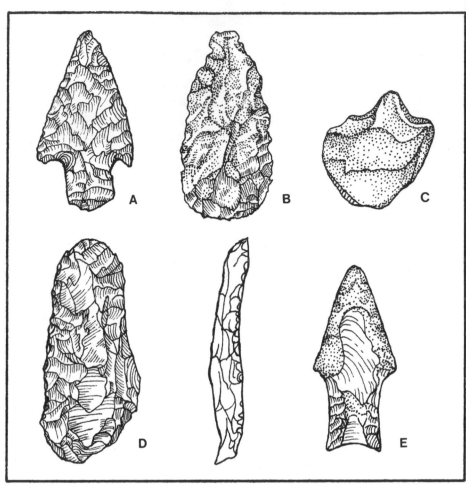

El Inga tools included the long-stemmed point (A), the leaf-shaped point (B), the graver (C), the uniface knife (D), and the fish-tailed point with a fluted base (E).

years of Paleolithic times, migrations occurred from Asia to the New World.

We must be cautious drawing too many firm conclusions from the finds at El Inga. Although similar points have shown up in many sites in both hemispheres, there are hundreds of other sites where these point-making styles and techniques were apparently unknown. This opens the way for other explanations for the finds at El Inga, and it raises some questions that archeologists will probably never be able to answer fully.

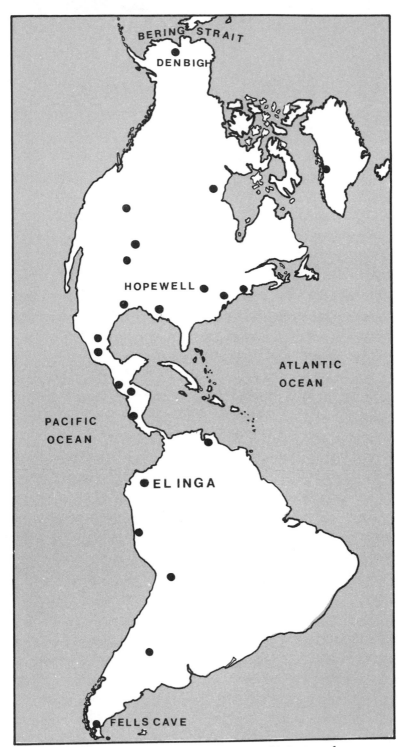

Stone age traditions were long lasting and widely spread as
shown by the distribution of El Inga tool-making styles.

Just how did skills and traditions spread? Did they simply pass from one neighboring tribe to the next? Or did one tribe, perhaps one wave of migration, dispersing into various regions of the land, leave widely scattered but commonly held skills and traditions? Or did similar traditions develop in separate regions independently without aid of contact?

Most archeological relics only hint at the answers. At Onion Portage, for instance, Dr. Anderson assumed different people moved into the region because of a complete change in the tool collections he found. It was probably a safe assumption, but the possibility that the earlier people remained cannot be completely ruled out. They might have changed their tool-making style to adopt to changing climatic conditions, and this might have happened with or without the influence of neighboring tribes.

We must also keep in mind that resistance to change varied from one culture to the next. The classic illustration of this varying resistance is the wheel, which was invented in both the Old and the New Worlds. In the Old World, the invention eased man's labors and speeded his transport in a spectacular fashion, but in the New World, the wheel served only as a curiosity and a plaything. Though many children's toys of pre-Columbian times rolled on wheels, there were no carts, wagons, or any other hauling devices that would have lightened the load for New World laborers.

The horse serves as another example. When Spanish explorers brought the modern horse to the New World, it revolutionized life for most Plains Indians. It provided swift travel and made it possible to hunt the vast herds of bison that roamed the Great Plains. Many Indians who had been living as farmers gave up their settled lives and became nomadic hunters. Horses, stolen, fought over, and bred with care, were the most highly prized possession for these Great Plains Indians. The Piute Indians, however, were an exception. Holding to their old hunting and gathering ways, the Piutes saw just one use for a horse. They ate it.

Thus change, even though it might seem logical, did not always happen. Certainly, New World natives would have benefited by putting the wheel to work, and the Piute would have improved his standard of living by riding instead of butchering the horse.

Indeed, among the many interpretations we can give to the collection of El Inga tools, one might illustrate further evidence of resistance to change. If the style represented there and elsewhere in widely scattered sites represents a single heritage that spread with a growing population, it is remarkable that the style changed so little. People living in different climates and habitats, separated for centuries, retained the same tool-making technique and style. They were ruled by a resistance to change.

Many other stone age sites show that this resistance to change was a dominant trait. At least one site shows that change, when it did come, was not always a change for the better.

Chapter Six

The Jungle's Secret

In Brazil's dense Amazon jungle, at a torrid place where the Galera River hooks toward the Bolivian frontier, a small band of Indians follow Stone Age traditions that began in the region perhaps fourteen thousand, five hundred years ago.

Until recently, little was known of this Stone Age band. It is the Wasúsus, part of a larger tribe, the Nambicauras, which has long been hostile to all white explorers. The native warriors, armed with spears and bows and arrows, have also accounted for the "disappearance" of many modern-day prospectors, lumbermen, and road builders who dared to enter the territory.

Even today, although their numbers have been greatly reduced by measles, influenza, and other diseases of civilization, the Nambicauras remain unpredictable. But with their bands reduced and widely scattered, the natives have been unable to hold back progress.

The Wasúsus band, now totalling no more than fifty-five men, women, and children, would have been lost to progress if it had not possessed a secret. The secret, guarded for generations, saved the Indians from the loss of their ancestral land and the loss of their identity as a distinct band.

Unlike most Nambicauras, Wasúsus do not live on the nearby highlands where the climate is milder and the country more open. Instead, they stay low in the river basin where both jungle growth and insects are thick and the weather is steaming hot.

Despite its uncomfortable living conditions, the land has valuable resources. The forest is crowded with rare, tropical woods that would bring top prices in the world markets. The ground holds a wide variety of minerals, and the land itself, once cleared, would produce rich yields for farmers. Thus, it was inevitable that the Brazilian government marked the Wasúsus' territory for development. The Indians, according to the government plan, would have to move to a reservation in the highlands.

The government decision came as devastating news for the Wasúsus. Even though the reservation was just a day's march away, the land and the climate there were completely different, and worst of all, the government rules and the influence of other reservation Indians would destroy Wasúsus ways and traditions. Although inexperienced and shy about dealing with the outside world, the Indians were desperate. They turned to a white man for help.

W. Jesco von Puttkamer, known to natives throughout the Amazon as *Borbula* or "man with the great moon face," is a writer and photographer who has spent many years studying, traveling among and writing about the Indians. Time and again, his interest in the tribes won their friendship, and it also won respect from officials of the Brazilian government who were anxious about the preservation of native populations. Many of the expeditions that took von. Puttkamer into the jungle had been financed by the government. It was on one of these expeditions, in 1970, that he first met the Wasúsus.

He was fascinated by this primitive, unspoiled tribe, and he was charmed by their innocence and their friendliness. Von Puttkamer returned again and again to the bend in the Galera River to make a thorough study of Wasúsus traditions.

Although they grow some corn, the Indians basically are hunters and gatherers. Their bows shoot a long-shafted arrow, and with it they can bring down the swift red deer. They also use their bows to shoot an arrow with a special blunt point that travels accurately under water, enabling the bowman to stun and take fish. Other delicacies in the Wasúsus diet include armadillo, cooked in its shell, tapir, crocodile tail, and the vampire bat.

Chief in their religion is the god of thunder, and they believe that some places in the forest are sacred. The men of the tribe meet on special occasions to play bamboo flutes. Women are banned from these events, and women are never allowed to see the flutes.

This, according to legend, was not always the case. The men told von Puttkamer that many years ago women alone had custody of the flutes. This was at a time when women warriors raided other tribes for men, killing some and taking others prisoner. When the women were finally overthrown, the men became the warriors and took possession of the bamboo flutes. The tale sounded something like the classic legend of the Amazons, and undoubtedly, it was such tales that gave the great Amazon River its name.

During one of his visits, von Puttkamer learned of the Wasúsus' plight. A young woman called Barbara, serving as spokesman for the band, told him that if he would agree to help them, she would lead him to secret places known to no other white man. The places, Barbara said, would prove the band's ancestral right to its land.

Von Puttkamer agreed at once. During the next few days, Barbara and her husband, Vaiôco, solemnly led the way along shaded trails to the sacred places. They were all rock shelters, apparent shrines protected by overhanging ledges and often hidden by dense jungle growth. The rock walls inside had been carved with many strange designs, but the most surprisisg things appeared on the dusty shelter floors. Fragments of well-designed pottery, hundreds of them, lay scattered before von Puttkamer's eyes.

Pottery making is an unknown art among the Wasúsus and most of today's other Amazon Indians. But these shelters appeared to have been pottery factories. Now, people who had lost the potter's art used the shelters for worship. Barbara and Vaiôco would not describe any of the worship ritual, but they clearly wanted von Puttkamer to know that the shelters were sacred places.

The largest shelter seemed to hold the most promise for excavation. Sunbursts—disks with many rays—and rising suns—half-circles crowned with rays—dominated the wall carvings here, and for this reason von Puttkamer called it Abrigo do Sol or "Shelter of the Sun."

When he returned to civilization, von Puttkamer went at once to the Catholic University of Goiás where he reported his discoveries to two archeologists. The professors received the news with excitement and surprise. At any dig, the presence of pottery often meant a farming culture.

As soon as arrangements could be completed, von Puttkamer led the two university archeologists to the site. Test trenches were sunk in the floor of Abrigo do Sol, and after just a few days of digging, the archeologists came to a firm conclusion. The site was not only worthy of an extensive excavation, but it also appeared clear that the Wasúsus did indeed have a strong ancestral claim to the land.

The initial report from the archeologists brought interest and financial backing for a full scale dig from the National Geographic Society. Later, the Smithsonian Institution gave its sponsorship. Meanwhile, the Brazilian government began to reconsider its order relocating the Wasúsus.

Unfortunately, a decision did not come before the Indians were packed off to the reservation, and crews of road builders and lumbermen moved into the territory. Giant trees crashed to the ground. Chain saws quickly sectioned them into logs, and trucks hauled the logs off to sawmills. Underbrush was burned to complete the clearing work.

Before too many acres were laid bare, however, the government acted. All work was halted. The crews were ordered out of the region, and the land was returned to the Wasúsus forever.

The Indians came home at about the same time that Eurico Miller of the Archeological Museum of the State of Rio Grande do Sol arrived to take charge of the excavation. With von Puttkamer's help, the natives were enrolled and organized into crews for the dig.

It was lucky the natives were available. No other workers would have lasted in the clouds of stinging insects and the heat. Even the hardy Indians had difficulty putting up with conditions at the dig. The dust of the shelter floor, composed mostly of powdered bat guano, rose in choking clouds wherever the crews worked. They coughed and choked and rubbed tears from their eyes, but they did work. Slowly they exposed layer after layer of human habitation.

Early in the dig, the workers came upon the skeleton

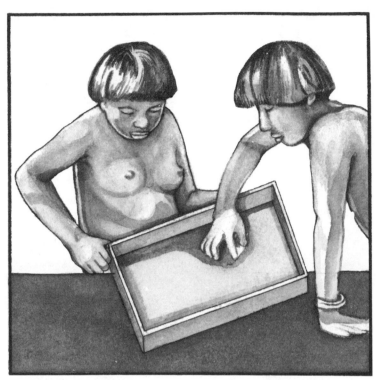

Native workers screen soil dug from the floor of Abrigo do Sol to make sure no artifact is overlooked.

of a child. Because bones decompose rapidly in the jungle's acid soil, this had to be a recent burial. Other fast decomposing organic material such as snail shells, bones of deer and wild pigs, corncobs, and fragments of bamboo arrow shafts were also listed as fairly recent material. One of the most exciting finds early in the dig was a piece of gold, but this too was recent. In fact, it looked like part of a necklace or earring similar to modern native jewelry.

Far more significant were the pottery fragments that appeared by the thousands in the upper layers. The fragments showed remarkable variety in technique and design. Some designs had been etched in the clay with a sharp stick while the clay was still wet. Other designs were made by applying ridges of clay to the pot before it was fired. There were some designs that combined both techniques.

Birds and animals were depicted. Strange human faces

Footprints, masks, fertility symbols, sunbursts, animals and abstract designs are depicted in wall carvings, while the pottery of Abrigo do Sol (bottom) showns advanced designing techniques.

also appeared. The native workers explained that these represented masks worn by witch doctors during rituals. Miller, however, was not sure if the natives really knew what the ancient potters were trying to depict. The skill and artistry shown in the fragments was far above the skill and artistry of the Wasúsus. How could they explain the designs with any authority?

Cylinders of pottery among the fragments were apparently used to roll out and flatten moist clay before forming it into pots. The cylinders suggest that the shelter may indeed have been a pottery workshop. Unfortunately, because of the fast decay of organic substances, no firm evidence appeared to show what kinds of food the pottery makers ate, or even whether they lived by farming, or by hunting and gathering.

In lower levels of the dig, the pottery fragments gave way to stone tools, many of them simply crude flakes. Unworked river stones also came to light. Apparently, they had been carried to the shelter as raw material for tool making, but had later been discarded and forgotten. The unworked stone led Miller to suspect that the shelter may have served, at least for a time, as a temporary camp, a place where wandering hunters stopped for the night or waited out a storm. They made tools or scratched designs on the shelter walls simply to pass the time.

Although sunbursts dominate the collection of wall carvings, another common design represents the human foot. Again, the Wasúsus had an explanation. The foot mark was simply a way of saying, "I was here." It was, the natives said, a sort of signature.

Another design, often repeated on the walls, is the symbolic sketch of female private parts. A triangular pattern, this symbol has been found at many other Stone Age sites in both the Old and New Worlds. It is generally interpreted as a fertility symbol, but von Puttkamer takes the frequency of the symbol at Abrigo do Sol as further support for the old Amazon legend. Women, he thinks, once played the dominant role in the lives of the people. Miller, however, with typical scientific caution, looks upon this as too fanciful an interpretation of the evidence.

Among the large boulders that have fallen from the roof of the shelter is one that bears many designs and deep grooves. The Wasúsus say it was a ritual stone, but they will not describe the ritual. Perhaps they don't know what it might have been. Could the boulder have served as a platform for human sacrifice? Grooves were sometimes carved in sacrificial stones as blood troughs, but Miller says these grooves might be nothing more than hone marks left by hunters when they sharpened their stone points and knives.

Dating of the carvings is difficult, but by good luck, charcoal samples were found in every level of habitation. With Carbon 14 dating, Miller was able to establish an accurate chronicle that gave the age of each level.

The oldest firm age found so far comes from the lowest level. A hunter's fire burned there twelve thousand years ago. Another lump of charcoal has been given an age of fourteen thousand five hundred years. Miller suspects that the date may be wrong, that there was either a laboratory error or that the charcoal went through a chemical change that produced a false reading. His main cause for suspicion is that this charcoal came from above the lowest level, but the age itself is also cause for doubt.

So far, the oldest evidence of human occupation in South America comes from sites in Peru and Venezuela, where Carbon 14 dating has given an age of thirteen thousand years. If the oldest date on Abrigo do Sol charcoal is ever accepted, it will push the beginning of the Stone Age in South America back by fifteen hundred years.

One difficulty at Abrigo do Sol is erosion. Heavy rains can wash away and mix together the material from different levels. Flooding may have caused the oldest sample of charcoal to appear out of place, but there is no way to prove that such a thing happened.

Another difficulty at the dig, one that eventually brought work there to a halt, is caused by fallen boulders. Too big to move without heavy machinery, the boulders rest upon soil that may hold deeper, older layers of human relics. But until money can be found to bring in the machinery, further exploration must be delayed.

After being stopped by boulders at Abrigo do Sol, Miller and his native crews investigated thirteen other sites, including some long-abandoned villages. In three seasons of digging, they collected 8,960 pottery fragments and 8,500 stone relics.

All the finds, according to the Wasúsus, were left by a people who were killed off centuries ago, but again, Miller is not sure. The stone chippers and the pottery makers might or might not have been direct ancestors of the modern band. In any case, it is hard to explain why pottery making in the region ceased. Certainly the Wasúsus could make good use of pottery for food storage, cooking, and serving bowls, but today they have no more concept of how pottery can be used than they do of how it might be made.

Why was the pottery-making art lost and forgotten? The mystery may never be solved. Certainly, Abrigo do Sol has not yet yielded all its secrets.

Chapter Seven

Meadowcroft

As the thread of smoke rose, the people around the hearth continued to stamp their feet and rub their hands. Even though they were sheltered here from the wind, the evening cold cut through the animal hide of their cloaks like spears.

Small flames snapped at the wood. Slowly, they grew. They danced. Then at last, the fire began to crackle merrily and give warmth.

When the flames cast the people's shadows high against the wall of the shelter, the preparations began. Meat from the day's hunt was set to roast. Wild walnuts were cracked and sorted. A collection of hackberries was divided carefully in the light of the fire. Then, the people settled down to eat.

Such a scene, or one much like it, occurred sixteen thousand years ago. Continental ice still covered more than half of North America, and at this place, in western Pennsylvania, the front wall of the ice mass was just fifty miles away.

The place, like Abrigo do Sol, is a rock shelter, but

unlike the Amazon site, this shelter has withheld few secrets from probing archeologists.

The ancient Ice Age camp, known today as Meadowcroft Rockshelter, is halfway up the sloping valley wall of Cross Creek and not far from the modern town of Avella. The shelter takes its name from Meadowcroft Village, a nineteenth century community owned and restored by Albert Miller. The village, a tourist attraction, stands at the rim of the valley above the shelter.

Exploring the slope beneath his village, Miller came upon the shelter in 1968. He could not claim discovery because the floor of the shelter was littered with beer cans and charcoal of recent fires. Hunters who track the migrating deer up and down Cross Creek had obviously known about the Shelter for many years.

The area is famous for its hunting because the valley provides one of the few easy routes for herds of deer to move north each season into the high browsing lands of Pennsylvania. Miller suspected that prehistoric hunters may have enjoyed the same kind of luck that the modern hunters do. He also suspected that prehistoric hunters, like those of today, may have found shelter beneath the rock overhang.

The shelter impressed Miller greatly. About three hundred square feet were protected by the overhanging ledge. Inside, the earth was remarkably dry, and even on a gusty day, the air was surprisingly still. Hunters could not have asked for a better camping place.

When Miller told members of the anthropology department at the University of Pittsburgh about the shelter, he caused a stir. Rock shelters are rare in the eastern United States, and here was one just thirty miles from the university. Obviously, it should be investigated at once.

Preliminary inspection of Meadowcroft, however,

convinced the experts that excavation must be slowly and carefully organized so that all the available resources of modern science could play a part in evaluating the site. Botanists must be enlisted to identify seeds and make microscopic study of pollens. Zoologists must be assigned the task of identifying and cataloguing bones. University computers should receive and store all data in a permanent record, made available to all. And of course, workers must be found and trained to take on the difficult chore of the excavation itself. A special man was needed to take charge, and the university found him, a special man indeed.

Dr. James M. Adovasio is an archeological prodigy. He learned to read at the age of four. When he was seven, he was poring through books on history and geology that would have been difficult reading for the average teenager. As soon as he discovered archeology books, he knew what his life work would be.

He joined his first dig while he was a student at the University of Arizona. He was just nineteen. In 1973, when he was picked to take charge at Meadowcroft, he was still a young man, short and muscular, with a jet-black beard—a thirty-year-old dynamo.

It was decided that work at the shelter would be limited to the school's summer holiday. With this schedule, archeology students from the university could do the work without losing time in the classroom. But the dig itself would be no holiday.

Work would start daily at 6 A.M.; Mondays through Fridays, the crew would stay on the job until 6 p.m.; on Saturdays, the workers could quit at noon, and they could take Sundays off.

None of the eighteen students on the dig seemed to be bothered by the heavy workload. They were inspired by Dr. Adovasio's enthusiasm and energy, and he had energy to spare. At the end of each work day, he climbed to his tent in the camp at the rim of the valley, fed his pet iguana, and then lifted weights for an hour before sitting down to dinner.

Despite the heavy work schedule, progress at the dig was slow. Every bit of earth, removed with small trowels and brushes, had to be sifted through fine screens. At each level, earth samples had to be collected frequently, packaged, and labeled and then sent to the university for analysis. Of course, any organic material, such as bone, wood, or charcoal, also had to be packaged and labeled and sent off to a laboratory for dating.

Workers at Meadowcroft faced the same problem that confronted the excavators of Abrigo do Sol. Huge boulders that had fallen from the roof of the shelter could not be moved. They hampered the step-by-step excavation of the shelter floor. Even small rocks could not be lifted until all the earth around them had been removed and sifted.

Dr. Adovasio was not discouraged. He urged everyone to work slowly and methodically. No single worker, he said, should expect to remove more than half a cubic meter of soil in a season. Care was the watchword. For it was abundantly clear by now that Miller's suspicions were correct. The shelter had been a prehistoric campsite for thousands of years.

There seemed to be no end to the record. Layer after layer yielded stone tools, bone fragments, lumps of charcoal, plant seeds, and shells. The bones, many scarred by stone knives, showed that the people hunted deer, elk, fox, cougar, bobcat, bear, and several different rodents. The people were as resourceful in gathering food as they were in hunting it. They ate seeds, berries, fruits, and perhaps even the shoots and leaves of some plants. The early Meadowcroft residents filled out their diet with shellfish.

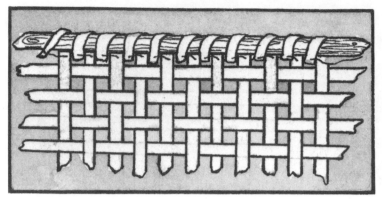

Simple but effective, Meadowcroft baskets were made of woven bark strips attached to a wooden rim.

Two of the most fascinating first season finds were a collection of domestic bean seeds and the remains of a basket woven out of tree bark. Both seemed very old, but the season was almost over before the Carbon 14 reports began coming back from the laboratory.

The beans were at least two thousand three hundred years old, older than any age yet suspected for the start of agriculture in the eastern United States. The basket was four thousand years old, again far older than any baskets previously found in the region.

It was not the age of individual relics that caused the greatest excitement among the workers at Meadowcroft. It was the entire chronicle of ages. By the end of the season, Dr. Adovasio realized that the site was an archeologist's dream. Here was a record of human occupation that stretched from 1265 A.D. back to 11,000 B.C. And the occupation appeared to be continuous. Hunters and their families camped in the shelter year after year.

There were a few gaps in the record, but Dr. Adovasio expected these would be filled in when some of the occupation levels beneath the boulders could be revealed. He also expected that digging in subsequent seasons would bring even older relics to light.

His expectations were realized during the next three summers. The student crew dug to an occupation level that has been assigned an age, through Carbon 14 dating, of sixteen thousand years. The traces of bark unearthed below this level hint at even a greater age. Unfortunately, there is not enough of the bark for testing, but if it were gathered by human hands for basket-making, it is possible that occupation of Meadowcroft began some nineteen thousand years ago.

The wealth of material yielded by Meadowcroft is impressive. At the end of the summer of 1977, after four full seasons of digging and two-thirds of the shelter floor excavated, the crews had found a hundred and sixty-two hearths. Many of them were on soil that had been discolored by heat. In addition, twenty-nine separate storage or refuse piles, rich in seed, shell, and bone, were discovered.

Bones and bone fragments total 211,818 and represent sixty-five different animals. There are seeds of at least fifty

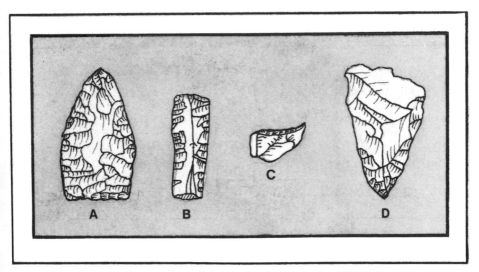

Typical Meadowcroft tools include a biface point (A), a simple blade (B), a microengraver, (C), and a knife (D).

different edible plants and shells of thirty-one different freshwater mollusks and bivalves.

More than thirteen thousand stone tools have been taken from the site. Many of the oldest tools in the collection are similar to the biface disks found at Onion Portage and on the shores of Lake Baikal in central Siberia.

In all, the dig has produced such a wealth of relics and information that it has put a serious strain on the resources of the scientists at the University of Pittsburgh. It will take several years to work on the soil samples alone. Minute organic material such as plant fibers and pollen must be extracted from the soil through floatation. Under this process, which is relatively new, soil is placed in a tank of special solution. The tank is agitated to bring the organic material to the surface, where it is collected, separated, and prepared for study. Although this work takes time, it is expected to produce the most detailed and fullest records of prehistoric vegetation and climate ever amassed in the New World.

Other phases of the study have already provided some remarkable details. The computer recording the types and locations of stone tools, for instance, apparently confirmed a division of labor among stone age people that was long suspected.

Dr. Joel Gunn, the computer analyst for the dig, noticed in the computer read-outs that the best tools, often those made of rare stones not native to the region, were invariably found near the front or open side of the shelter. Poorer tools made of local stone were found at the back of the shelter. This pattern persisted, virtually unchanged, on levels dated from nine thousand to twelve thousand years of age.

Without the computer, this pattern might have gone unnoticed. Of course, the computer could not explain the pattern, but Dr. Gunn put forth a plausible theory. He believes that the men in the group had their work areas at the shelter entrance. Here they could guard their families and keep an eye out for game. The women, who probably had the chores of butchering meat, scraping hides, and sorting the seeds, nuts, and berries they had gathered, had their work areas in the inner, more protected areas of the shelter. The women, with their domestic cares, including the care of the children, could not roam far in search of the better quality stones for their tools. The men, on the other hand, traveling on the trail of game, had the chance to search out and perhaps even trade for high quality stones. The tool pattern thus suggests that Stone Age women were far from liberated and it could be inferred that Stone Age men ruled the family and, perhaps, thereby avoided many of the more tedious and demanding chores.

Other insights into the Stone Age life at Meadowcroft will undoubtedly emerge as testing of the material and processing of the data continues. Meanwhile, at the end of the 1977 season, Dr. Adovasio ordered work at the site halted for at least ten years.

His decision will allow the testing and processing of material already collected to be completed, but there is another good reason for the halt. The project director believes that in ten years American archeology will be greatly changed. Not only will more sophisticated methods and techniques be available, but also archeologists themselves may be asking a whole new set of questions about the past. Thus, Dr. Adovasio wants the remaining, unexcavated third of the shelter floor at Meadowcroft preserved untouched until the late 1980s.

From the material already collected and processed, however, we can say that Stone Age life at Meadowcroft was surprisingly rich and varied. The people did not depend on hunting alone. They could get food from many different plants, and they knew how to find and collect a wide assortment of shellfish. The variety of their resources suggests that they rarely went hungry. Their talent for diversity, thus, kept their larders full. Other Stone Age people, those who specialized, did not apparently enjoy the same bounty. These were the big game hunters.

Chapter Eight

The Extinction Mystery

Imagine most of what is now Canada still covered with ice and think of the rest of North America as a vast carpet of green, dotted with blue lakes and etched with many rivers. Because of the ice melt and because of much higher rainfall than we have today, the lakes were vast and the rivers were mighty. Some of the lakes—Lake Mannix, for instance—filled the huge basins that have since become deserts. With abundant water, vegetation was lush. Generally, the eastern half of the continent was covered thickly with forests of conifers and hardwood trees, while the Great Plains and the foothill valleys of the Rockies and Sierra Nevada rippled with tall grasses.

If you can imagine such conditions, you will have a fair picture of how North America appeared some thirteen thousand years ago, 1100 B.C., when the ice sheets began their final retreat. To complete the picture, however, you

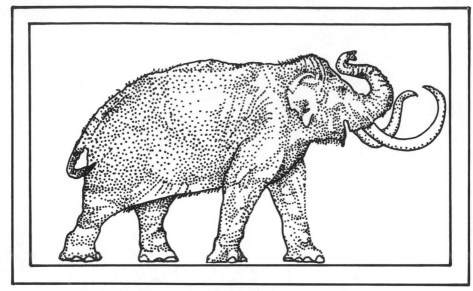

The Columbia mammoth stood twelve feet high at the shoulders and weighed several tons, an awesome quarry for Stone Age hunters.

must also envision many animals, some of them so huge and unusual that they challenge the imagination.

The giant ground sloth, with a small head and sharp claws, was almost the size of an elephant. There was a cave bear that stood taller than any bear known today. Mammoths, bigger than any modern elephant, roamed the Great Plains. The wooly mammoth had long, coarse hair that trailed almost to the ground. The Columbia mammoth was just as big, but had short hair. Both were armed with powerful trunks and curving tusks that made awesome weapons. The mastodon, slightly smaller with shorter tusks, was a forest elephant and lived mostly in the eastern half of the continent. There was also the pigmy mammoth that left its bones at the apparent kill site on Santa Rosa Island.

The several kinds of bison included a long-horned species that was twice the size of the American bison of modern times. Horses also came in several shapes and sizes. One was no bigger than a collie dog, while others stood much higher than any horse known today. There were camels, tapirs, giant armadillos, and several different antelopes, including a four-horned species. Although there were giant carnivores such as the dire wolf and saber-toothed tiger, most of the Ice Age or Pleistocene mammals were grass eaters, and like most grass-eating animals, they moved in herds across the valleys and the plains. They numbered in the millions.

Today's forty-eight contiguous states of the United States, it has been estimated, once supported seventy-five million animals, each with an average weight of one thousand pounds. North American animals thus once attained a greater population and greater individual size than found today in any African game preserve.

What happened to all these animals? Here is the great mystery of the Pleistocene Epoch.

In just eight thousand years, from fifteen thousand to seven thousand years ago, the horse, the elephant, the camel and twenty-eight other genera in the animal kingdom vanished from the New World. Among the large grazers, only the American bison of the Great Plains and the musk ox of the high Arctic survived. Of all others, only bones remain.

For many years, a prevailing theory held that climatic changes caused the mass extinction. Rainfall diminished, rivers shrank, lakes dried up, and the rich expanses of grass diminished. The change, according to this theory, reduced the food supply so much that the animals simply died off.

A few experts took exception to the theory. It seemed unlikely to them that a change of climate alone would cause the complete extinction of such a great variety of animals, but alternate theories were harder to accept. One notion had it that winters turned colder, killing off newly born animals, but these were the hardy animals that thrived all during the Ice Age. Another notion suggested that epidemics swept through the land, but it is hard to believe that a disease could be carried by so many different animals and prove fatal to them all.

Could human beings have caused the extinction? For many years the hunting theory on extinction of the animals had little support. A mammoth, after all, stood twelve feet high at the shoulders, weighed several tons, and could defend itself ably with its trunk and tusks. The herds of grazing animals were swift and not inclined to give an unmounted spearman an easy target. Even after archeological discoveries early in this century showed that Stone Age hunters were indeed able to kill the huge animals, the hunting theory was generally shunned.

Today, however, with a wealth of evidence carefully gathered over many years, there is a growing belief that Stone Age hunters played a major role in the extinction. Still, the hunting theory is not without complications.

For instance, we know that men hunted the Pleistocene animals in both the Old World and the New. In fact, many more kill sites have been discovered in Europe and Asia than in North and South America. Yet elephants, camels, and horses, wiped out in the New World, survived in the Old World.

Does this mean that New World animals were less wary and thus easier to stalk than the animals of the Old World? Or does it mean that New World hunters were more efficient killers than Old World hunters? Backers of the hunting theory say yes to both questions.

The large animals were less wary because up until the close of the Ice Age the few humans who occupied the New World did not prey heavily on them. Although the early Americans lacked the skill and the weapons to take the big game, they were successful in hunting smaller animals such as the deer, fox, bobcat, possum, and rabbit. According to the theory, this explains why the small animals survived. They learned fear as soon as humans arrived in the New World. The larger animals, rarely bothered, remained without fear.

Thus, when hunters gained the ability and developed the weapons to kill big game, the destruction was swift and complete. This conclusion, however, raises another question that long challenged the hunting theory of extinction. Just what new ability and what new weapons allowed hunters to prey so successfully on big game? The answer has emerged slowly.

In 1932, when unique spear points were found among mammoth bones at a site near Clovis, New Mexico, most archeologists suspected a hoax. The discovery, after all, occurred at a time when it was generally believed that people arrived in the New World by boat, long after all the Pleistocene animals were extinct. The spear points could not be related to any other points yet seen.

They were well-shaped, rather heavy points with a flat or concave base. But the feature that made them unique was fluting. Both sides, from the base up to about the middle had been hollowed out. Evidently each hollow or flute was accomplished with a single, well-placed blow struck at the base of the point.

Experts who examined the Clovis site and believed that the points were authentic said that the fluting might have been done to increase flow of blood from a wound, but it seemed more likely that fluting served to give a tighter fit in hafting the point to the spear. A tight haft without a large bulge of binding material would allow the thrusted spear to sink deep into flesh, increasing the chance for a fatal wound. This explanation, as it turned out, was a good guess.

It took years, however, for the Clovis discoveries to gain general acceptance. Only after similar kill sites were found near Dent, Colorado; Miami, Texas; Dombo, Oklahoma; Mockingbird Gap, New Mexico; and Murry Springs, Naco, Escapule, and Leikem, all in Arizona, did it become abundantly clear that people not only shared the land with the Pleistocene animals, but that hunters also preyed upon them with great success.

Other facts emerged. The Clovis hunters were specialists. Their points, almost always associated with mammoth kills, showed that the mammoth was their prime quarry. Most kill sites were located at ancient water holes. The hunters evidently waited in ambush and attacked the huge beasts to drive them into the water and mud where their movements were restricted. Usually the spearmen took female or young animals and avoided the larger, fiercer bulls.

The mammoths were butchered where they fell, and it appeared that the hunters and their families camped at the kill site until most of the meat was consumed. Then, they moved on. The elephants, by leaving trails across the grassy tracks, led the hunters to the next promising ambush.

We can assume that the hunters moved in small bands, perhaps no more than large family units, and with their nomadic ways, they could carry little with them. The only relics they left at the kill sites seemed to be their fluted points and a few stone scrapers and knives. But there was another relic that was generally overlooked in the original examination of the sites. Straight shafts of bone found at the kill sites were usually dismissed as crude scrapers. The shafts, about ten inches long and tapered at both ends, served a more deadly purpose. Discovery of this purpose, however, did not come until later.

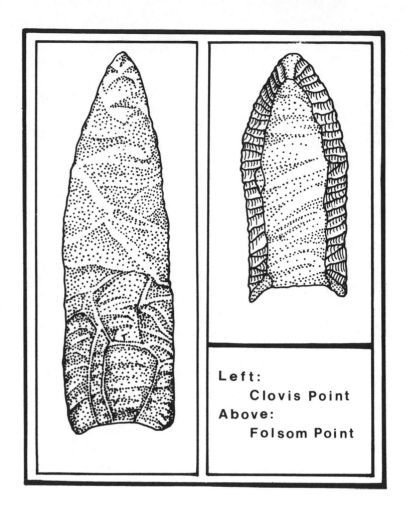

Left:
   Clovis Point
Above:
   Folsom Point

Meanwhile, as Clovis sites were being found and excavated, other, much different kill sites came to light. One of the first of these was found near Folsom, New Mexico, where a new kind of fluted point appeared among the scattered bones of giant bison. Folsom points, as they are now called, provide the finest example of the stone worker's art. Indeed, it took modern day students of the art ten years to learn how to duplicate a Folsom point.

The points, smaller and more delicate than Clovis points, are finely shaped and fluted with such symmetry that their edged rims are equal in width from base to point. The edges themselves are flaked with machine-like exactness and uniformity. Is a Folsom point something more than a weapon? Yes. It is puzzling, but the points were definitely made better than they had to be. They were works of art.

It seems that the Folsom craftsmen were motivated by pride. They wanted to produce an object of beauty, something that would provide a lasting testament of their skill.

While the points may have been works of art to their makers, the hunters knew how to put the points to practical use. Folsom hunters were highly efficient killers of the giant bison.

The efficiency was due partly to hunting methods. Because bison could be stampeded into blind canyons or over cliffs they died by the hundreds in a single hunt. An animal injured in a fall or simply cornered and confused was an easy target for the spear.

Driving a herd of animals required organization and planning, and this meant leadership. Some of the hunters had to be counted on to start the herd running. Still others had to be positioned along the path of the stampede to prevent the frightened animals from turning off their intended path. Then, at the end, the spearmen had to be positioned so they would have the best angles of attack.

Hunting in this manner required many people, but a successful hunt, one that might drive an entire herd to destruction, produced a bounty of fresh meat. Division of the meat, undoubtedly, called again for leadership. We can assume the Folsom hunters moved in large, well-organized bands. A band may have scattered between hunts, but whenever a herd of bison was sighted, it would be necessary to gather and organize again to assure a successful drive.

Possibly drives were started by setting grass fires downwind from the herd. This could have saved some manpower, but in the long run, too many fires in one area would destroy the feed and force the bison to seek other pastures. We can't say for sure, but the hunters were probably intelligent enough to understand the harmful result of grass fires. Just the same, some experts have suggested that man-made fires hastened the extinction of the grazing herds by depleting their feed.

When Carbon 14 dating became available it was found that Clovis people hunted mammoths from ten thousand nine hundred to some fifteen thousand years ago with peak activity in the last six hundred years of that period. Folsom hunters were stampeding herds of giant bison from nine thousand to eleven thousand years ago. Clovis and Folsom people were not the only ones who hunted the big game. Scandia hunters, who used a spear point with an offset hafting stem at the base to kill mammoths and perhaps other big game, preceded Clovis hunters by several thousand years. Thus far, however, few Scandia relics have been discovered.

On the more recent end of the time scale were hunters with a variety of unfluted stone points who tracked both the giant and the modern bison, antelope, and other big game up until about seven thousand five hundred years ago. By then, however, most of the Pleistocene animals had vanished.

For a long time, the experts could not understand why different species of Pleistocene animals died off at different times. The pygmy elephant vanished twelve thousand years ago. The wooly mammoth disappeared some ten thousand years ago. Two species of large bison died off about eight thousand years ago. The horse, camel, and columbian mammoth followed the large bison by about five hundred years. The mastodon hung on until just six thousand years ago. The climatic change theory failed to explain the phenomena, but an explanation could be found in the hunting theory.

The hunters were specialists. They concentrated on one species and continued hunting that species until it died off. Then, new specialists arrived or evolved to hunt a different species. Thus, according to the hunting theory, the mastodon enjoying the cover of forested regions was the last to fall to specialized hunting.

Archeologists put all the big game specialists in the classification of the Paleo-Indian tradition. For many years it was a tradition known almost entirely by kill sites and the sketchy remains of temporary camps. Burial sites were strangely absent from the record, but then, in 1968, during construction work on a hillside near Wilsall, Montana, a cluster of human bones appeared in the scoop of an earth-loading machine. The machine had broken into a grave that once lay beneath a rock overhang. Long ago, the rock overhang collapsed, but a thin layer of soil had protected the grave.

Archeologists rushed to the site and began a complete and careful excavation. They found the skeletons of two young adults and more than a hundred tools of flint and bone. Included in the collection were Clovis points.

An age of ten to eleven thousand years confirmed that here indeed was a Clovis burial site. Two exciting facts were revealed. The first was apparent at once. The Clovis hunters were a religious people, expecting life after death. Nearly all of the relics had been broken in the belief that the spirit of each tool or point would thereby be released to accompany the spirit of the dead into the afterlife. This custom, followed for centuries by Stone Age people, is still the practice of primitive tribes throughout the world. In addition, the bodies of the dead at the Wilsall site had been liberally covered with red ochre. This gave evidence of another old religious custom. Red stands for blood, rebirth, and renewal. It was symbolic of life and assured life after death. Thus, the burial site provided the earliest evidence yet discovered of religion in the New World.

The second fact was not so obvious. Among the broken relics found in the graves were the carefully shaped shafts of bone that had been previously noted only casually at Clovis kill sites. From their abundance, the shafts seemed to have equal significance with the flint points, but what purpose did they serve?

Two Canadian archeologists decided to find the answer. Larry Lahren of the University of Calgary in Alberta and Robson Bonnichsen of the Archeological Survey in Ottawa made a detailed study of shafts from the burial site and several kill sites. Their first conclusion was that the shafts were not scrapers.

Cut from the long bones of animals, the shafts had been straightened with a great deal of care. It appeared that they had first been softened in hot water and then bound to straight branches, or wedged between rocks to remove all natural curvature. One end of each shaft was evenly tapered, but the other had a shelf-like notch. All varied little from an average length of ten inches.

Lahren and Bonnichsen could draw but one conclusion. The bones were foreshafts, part of a Stone Age invention that was about as revolutionary to big game hunting as the machine gun was to modern warfare.

The shafts, with a point hafted to the notched end and the other end fitted into the socket of a wooden spear, were, in effect, lethal darts. With a strong thrust, such a dart could be buried deeply in the flesh, and it would remain embedded in the flesh when the hunter pulled his spear away. Then, by fitting another dart into the spear socket, the same hunter could wound his prey again.

The system allowed the hunter to travel lightly with

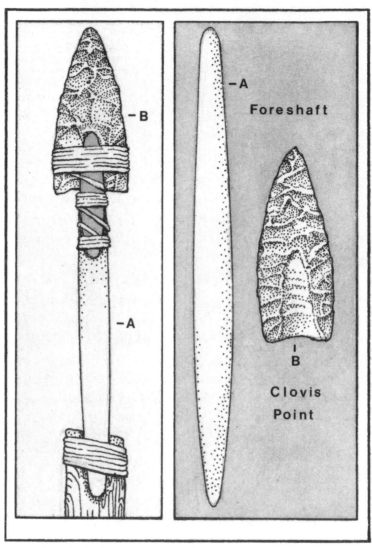

Bone foreshafts (A) and points (B), typical finds at Clovis kill sites, may have been man's first weapon of mass destruction. Drawing at the left shows how they were probably assembled and fitted to the end of a spear shaft.

just one wooden spear, but by carrying several darts, that spear could be rearmed again and again. Thus, the Clovis hunter was far more efficient than any hunters of the Old World. Today, some archeologists regard the Clovis dart as the first weapon of mass destruction. But was it responsible for the destruction of big game in the New World?

It was probably just partly responsible. Even strong advocates of the hunting theory of extinction concede that a drying trend in the climate restricted grazing territory for the animals, but this combined with advanced weapons and one other important factor spelled doom for the animals.

The other important factor may have been the world's first population explosion. In applying their skill and their weapons among unwary beasts, the hunters, with a seemingly boundless supply of meat, multiplied rapidly.

Paul S. Martin of the University of Arizona believes that a small band, perhaps numbering no more than a hundred souls, could have expanded to saturate North and South America in seventeen generations or about three hundred and forty years. All it would take would be an average population increase of 3.4 percent a year, and this rate, Martin believes, would be reasonable when food was plentiful and climate was mild. With such rapid growth, the demand for food would soar and over-hunting would diminish the herds at a frightening rate. If the growth Martin envisions did indeed occur, it is little wonder that the extinction of Pleistocene animals was swift and complete.

It must be remembered, however, that for all the recent support given the hunting theory, it remains just a theory. All we know for certain is that the animals did die off, and that the people who hunted them had to seek other sources of food. As we will see, people who grew to depend more and more on gathered foods—seeds, berries, leaves, and roots—eventually led the way to farming. Thus, we can say that the extinction of the animals sparked human progress.

There were other people, however, who moved to new hunting grounds. True the big game was gone, but smaller animals, fish, and fruits and berries were abundant. Life was good, too good for great progress, but some of these people reached the ultimate achievements in Stone Age craftsmanship.

Chapter Nine

Happy Hunting

While digging the foundations for his new house near the beach, a Newfoundland fisherman and his friends unearthed human bones from red-stained sand. The workers' shovels soon exposed several complete skeletons. Each lay in flexed position with knees drawn up to the rib cage. With the bones were stone tools and ornaments made of stone, shell, bone, and ivory. In all, the workers discovered eight graves.

The fisherman did not let the discoveries delay work on his house. It was the fall of 1967, and Labrador winds had already brought a sharp chill to the air. The fisherman wanted to move into his new home before the winter snows arrived.

Just the same, the unusual discoveries caused a great deal of talk, and before long, news of old graves found at the small village of Port au Choix on Newfoundland's Great Northern Peninsula reached the ears of archeologists. The report of the red-stained sand was particularly exciting. Port au Choix just might be a burial site for the mysterious Red Paint People.

At least a dozen other burial sites of these people had been located from Maine to Newfoundland and eastward into Ontario, but in almost all of these burials, natural acids in the soil had destroyed the bones and all other organic materials. The few stone tools and the red ocher that lined the grave pits did not give many clues to the nature of these people or how they lived. The lack of organic material made it impossible to date the graves. All that could be assumed was that the Red Paint People were part of the Archaic tradition, a culture that dominated eastern North America for the many centuries that followed big game hunting.

Archaic people, with no agriculture or pottery, were hunters and gatherers, but they were far more settled than the Paleo-Indian big game hunters. The Archaic Indians moved with the seasons in set patterns, visiting favorite berry patches for annual harvests, camping next to the same streams or lakes year after year for fish runs, and lying in wait on the same trails each spring for caribou or other migrating herds.

The Old Copper People of the upper Great Lakes, part of the Red Paint Tradition, had even stronger cause for stability. They had learned to work the copper from the native ores found along the shores of Lake Superior. Some craftsmen may have established permanent camps near these deposits.

With greater stability came the rise of religion. Use of red, symbolic of blood and life, in their burials was almost universal among the Archaic tribes. The practice, as we have seen from the discovery at Wilsall, was followed by at least some of the big game hunters. But we cannot say that Clovis hunters established the practice because red pigment has been found in ancient graves throughout the world. Use of red is simply the sign of a strong belief in life after death. Clovis hunters held this belief, and so did the Red Paint People of Archaic times.

How formal was the belief? How much did it dominate the people's lives? Without full and unspoiled grave relics, archeologists were unable to answer for the Red Paint People. Then came the news from Port au Choix.

Systematic exploration of the site was organized by the Memorial University of Newfoundland with James A. Tuck in charge. Financial support came from the Department of Provincial Affairs of the Canadian government and from the National Museum of Canada.

One happy fact came to light at once. Long ago, sea levels of the region had once been higher. The burials were in an old beach, nineteen feet above the present shore level, and because of shell deposits, the sandy soil had a high alkaline content, which neutralized natural acids. This was why the bones had survived through time.

It was unfortunate, of course, that the fisherman and his friends had removed eight skeletons from the site, but the university workers soon located another grave near the original discoveries. This was a double burial, containing the bodies of two women, and again the burial pit had been lined with red ocher. One body lay on its back with its lower legs bent under it at the knees. The other had been buried in a tightly flexed position, suggesting that the body had been wrapped in a shroud before burial.

The additional grave brought the total to ten bodies buried at the site. Only two of these proved to be men. One of the males unearthed by the house builders had a bundle of grave goods cradled in his arms.

For a time, the discoveries seemed to be over, but archeologists continued to search along the old beach. It was a mile long and ranged from thirty to seventy feet in width. The sand was capped by a layer of humus built up

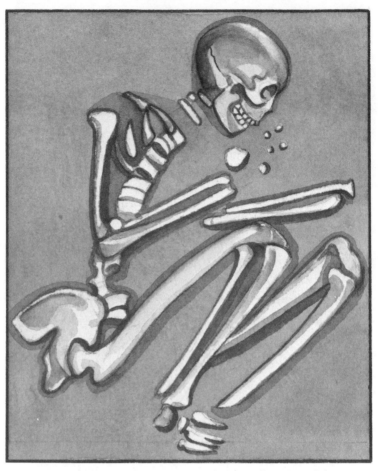

*The dead at Port au Choix were buried in a flexed position,
often with artifacts bundled in their arms.*

from the forest that had long covered the site, but beneath
the humus was sand, easy to dig even with crude tools. It
was an ideal location for Stone Age graves. Furthermore,
the beach faced eastward. Many other known burial sites
of the Archaic tradition also faced eastward, strongly suggesting worship of the rising sun.

The continued search was rewarded. Farther away
from the village, Tuck and his helpers found more burials,
many more.

Stones had been placed over most of the graves. They
may have been put there as markers, but their purpose

might have been mainly to discourage animals from digging up the bodies. In any case, the stones helped the archeologist locate a completely undisturbed cemetery. It proved to hold fifty-three graves.

The number alone was astounding. It put the Port au Choix site on record as the largest known Archaic cemetery. It turned out that many of the graves contained more than one skeleton. At the end of the excavation, Tuck could count the remains of almost a hundred complete skeletons and several more that were partially complete. With the bones were thousands of relics—hunting points, stone tools, ornaments, and some relics that seem to have been intended solely as funeral offerings.

Many of the burials were secondary ones which was not surprising in northern regions where the ground remains frozen during the winter months. When death occurred during the winter, the body was wrapped in a skin and left above ground until thawing weather made it possible to dig a grave pit. In some Port au Choix burials, disjointed and even incomplete skeletons suggested that decay was well advanced before the individuals received final interment.

Carbon 14 dating showed that the earliest burials were about four thousand four hundred years old, the latest about three thousand four hundred years old. These ages corresponded with skeletons found a thousand miles to the west in Ontario's Ottawa River valley, at one of the few other dated Archaic cemeteries.

The bones at Port au Choix showed that infant mortality among the Archaic Indians was high. Fifteen of the dead were less than two years of age. Twelve were newborn babies. Another fifteen were between six and eighteen years of age, and one was between eighteen and twenty-one. Thus, just half of the skeletons were adults, and of the adults only seven were more than fifty years old.

Although some skeletons showed evidence of arthritis in the spine or in finger joints, scientists were unable to determine causes of death. Most of the individuals seemed to have led healthy lives. Teeth showed heavy wear, probably from softening animal hides by chewing, but there was practically no evidence of tooth decay.

Dogs were also buried in the cemetery. We cannot say if dogs were trained to haul small loads, were used for hunting or retrieving, or simply as guard dogs. But it is a safe guess that they were buried as well-loved pets thought to have souls of their own that would pass on to the happy hunting grounds along with their owners.

Although the human and animal bones told much about these early hunters and gatherers, the artifacts included with the burials caused the greatest excitement among the archeologists. Finely made adzes and axes showed that the people were skilled woodworkers and almost certainly used this skill to build dug-out canoes. All the tools were remarkably well made.

Just one point in the collection was chipped in the old, Paleo-Indian manner. All others were made by grinding and polishing slate to form beautifully smooth weapons. So precise are the shapes and angles of some blades that they match modern designs forged in steel. Included among these are long, narrow blades that look like the bayonets of modern warfare.

It is likely that some of these long and thin blades were never used as weapons. They were instead intended as ornaments, a proud possession meant to be carried to the owner's grave.

Other sturdier blades, Tuck believes, were used to hunt caribou, probably during both the spring and fall migrations. Meat from the spring hunt could be preserved by drying. Meat taken in the fall could be preserved by freezing.

In summer, the main activities were probably fishing and berry picking. Salmon taken by spear or net could again be preserved by drying. In winter, boatmen went to the sea in quest of seals and possibly whales. Toggle harpoon points and shafts were common among the grave relics.

The toggle harpoon, known in all Arctic regions, was designed to come off the shaft after the point was thrust into the prey. Tension on the line, attached near the tip, pulled the point sideways and anchored it firmly in the flesh. Modern Eskimos still use this weapon to take seals.

The Archaic Indians at Port au Choix also made points toothed with fine barbs. They could have been used on marine mammals but were most likely used to harpoon fish.

Most daggers, needed to kill wounded animals, were fashioned out of caribou bones, but one was made of walrus ivory, and it may have been carried in a sheath that combined caribou antler and some perishable material. Only the antler portions of the sheath survived the long burial.

Decorative ornaments of bone pins and shells, animal teeth and claws, even birds' legs, apparently sewn to clothing, also survived while the skin clothing decayed. Some combs, fashioned out of caribou antler, bore delicately carved bird heads. One head is unmistakably that of a merganser. Another might be a swan, goose, or large-billed duck. A bone pin was carved with the head of the great awk, a bird that is now extinct.

Other items found in the grave offerings included a crude human figurine carved out of antler and a killer

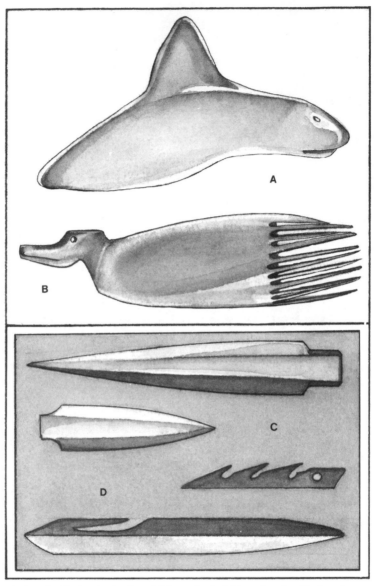

Animal effigies include a killer whale (A) and a duck's head carved in a caribou antler comb (B). Weapons include highly polished spear points (C) and barbed and unbarbed harpoons (D).

whale of polished stone showing the characteristic high dorsal fin. The human figure and the killer whale may have been used by a medicine man in religious ceremony.

In general, the grave offerings do not suggest a strong

class system. It seemed that each individual was buried with his or her own treasured ornaments and tools. A skilled woodworker, for instance, was buried with his stone axes and scrapers, a hunter with his spear points, and a hide worker with her needles. Tuck found that males often had the richest collection of artifacts, but this was not always the case.

Many of the ornaments suggest a belief in totems or good luck charms. When a duck was represented on a carved artifact, for instance, the legs of the same bird were sewn to the clothing. It may have been that these people simply thought that wearing the teeth or claws of an animal would bring luck in hunting it. It is also possible that these ornaments were clan or family symbols.

The use of red ocher, the alignment with the rising sun, and many broken or "killed" artifacts point to strong religious awareness at Port au Choix. Though not the earliest evidence of religion in the New World, the grave relics certainly show an enduring faith. The people followed the same traditions, the same unvaried burial rituals for more than a thousand years.

What ended this stable existence? The best answer is found in the study of the land in the region. What once were lakes are now bogs and meadows. Even streams that used to tumble clearly down rocky beds have slowed, filled with silt and turned boggy in leveled courses. This is a natural geological process in the aging of lakes and streams, but it destroyed fishing and brought enough change in vegetation to reduce food for game animals.

Thus, the people moved away. They probably headed south where lakes and rivers were slower to bog up. Some students of Indian cultures believe the people of Port au Choix were the ancestors of the great Algonquin Indians who were living in northeastern America when the colonists arrived. Algonquins, incidentally, broke relics before burying them with their dead.

We cannot say positively what became of these early Newfoundlanders. We only know that about three thousand years ago, they stopped using the beach at Port au Choix as a cemetery. And that's when the record there of the Red Paint People ends.

PART III

A Place in the Sun

MONK'S MOUND

POVERTY POINT

TEOTIHUACAN
TEHUACAN
VALLEY

GUAYAS PROVINCE

CHAN CHAN

CUSCO

Chapter Ten

New Horizons

For many years, right after spring plowing, a Southern Illinois farmer would spend a few hours of his busy day searching a neighbor's field for Indian relics. The field, at the north boundary of Theodore Koster's farm, was a rich source of spear and arrow points, and of course, the plowing brought new relics to light each spring.

The farmer's collection of relics grew steadily, and by 1969, it was impressive enough to attract the attention of archeologists from Northwestern University. In this manner the Koster site was discovered, and startling clues on human progress in the New World were eventually unearthed.

Essentially, Koster is a Stone Age site typical of Archaic traditions, but as we have already seen, Stone Age people were no strangers to progress. We can look upon the use of foreshafts as a new technology for Clovis hunters. The scratching of symbols on the walls of a rock shelter in the Amazon jungle can be regarded as a first step in development of a written language. Organization of a successful buffalo stampede might be said to mark the beginnings of central government. Making of relics for use as grave offerings only, and the breaking of these relics might record the first signs of both art and religion. An increase in the need for gathered food might well be cited as the beginning of agriculture.

Traditionally, the invention of agriculture stands as the dividing line separating the Stone Age from the modern era, but it is misleading to think in terms of strict dividing lines. For one thing, agriculture developed slowly over many thousands of years, and it must also be recognized that agriculture would not have come at all if the nomadic life didn't give way to a more settled existence. A settled life was the necessary preamble of human progress. It is the evidence of a settled life and its effect on Stone Age people that gives the Koster site its great significance.

Farmer Koster's field lies between a bend in the lower Illinois River and a sheltering rise of limestone cliffs. The site is just a few miles north of the Illinois' confluence with the Missouri River. In prehistoric times the rivers were fuller than today, and there were many lakes in the area. These waters provided good fishing and abundant shellfish harvest. The bottom land along the rivers was rich and moist, ideal soil for seed-bearing marsh plants. And on the bluffs above the cliffs, the forest began. Game there was plentiful, and several trees in the forest dropped edible nuts. For primitive people, the sheltered field invited permanence.

For archeologists, one of the first points of interest in the original collection of relics was the scarcity of pottery fragments. The scarcity suggested antiquity, a site that was occupied before the full development of the potter's art.

In the preliminary survey of the site, archeologists used a new device, a probing tool that consisted of a five-foot rod tipped by a hollow metal ball. Whenever the ball struck something solid in a test hole, it sent vibrations up the rod. Judging from the number of contacts with solid objects, it seemed that deposits of relics and bones lay deep and thick beneath the field. The ball of the probe was also equipped to bring up small samples of dirt from various levels in the test holes. Light-colored dirt indicated a sterile level with no human occupation, while dark dirt, rich in organic matter, was a sign of occupation.

In this manner, before disturbing the field, the archeologists were able to count twelve different levels of occupation. Later, two additional levels were identified. The site was richer than anyone had imagined. Planning for a full-scale excavation began at once.

Appointed to lead the project were Professors James A. Brown and Stuart Struever of Northwestern University and R. Bruce McMillan of the Illinois State Museum. They began marshalling all available resources for a dig to begin in the summer of 1970.

By good fortune there were many other archeological sites in the region, and for this reason, the Foundation for Illinois Archeology decided to establish a training center for archeological students at Kampsville, a small village little more than a stone's throw from the Koster Farm. The university and the foundation joined forces for the excavation of Koster. It was a happy partnership. Kampsville was open for students ages ten and older. The younger students would learn from observing the project while those at the college level would make up the work crews for the dig. University professors would teach at the training center, and at the same time, have access to the laboratories and living quarters there.

The partnership also led to broad financial support for the dig, with help ranging from modest contributions from many interested individuals to the substantial support of government grants. The excavation of Koster thus became a grass roots undertaking, and this, too, proved to be a stroke of good fortune. With no single agency governing the budget, the work was able to continue through the generosity of many different individuals and agencies even when costs increased. And the costs did increase beyond expectations. Sides of the excavation had to be shored up and protected from erosion. Before long it was necessary to install a mechanical conveyor to remove earth. Eventually, when work on the lowest levels began, pumps had to be installed to remove ground water. But as costs grew, so did the interest of contributors.

Today we can say that the expense was more than justified. Koster yielded valuable new knowledge, and in many cases this knowledge caused sharp revisions in our views of the past.

Like Onion Portage, Koster is a stratified site with the layers or horizons of occupation separated by soil that has washed down on the field periodically from the bluffs above. The sides of the dig look like a layer cake of dark and light soil, and it is a thick cake. The deepest layer to be investigated, called horizon thirteen, is thirty-seven feet below the present level of the field. Carbon 14 dating has given this horizon an age of nine thousand five hundred years.

Two feet above, in a thick layer of occupation, called horizon eleven, archeologists found remains of crude houses and other evidence of permanence such as stone slabs for grinding seeds, which could not easily be transported, and a cemetery. This level is seven thousand four hundred years old. Permanence, or at least semi-permanence, began far earlier than had been supposed.

Before the evidence of Koster came to light it was thought that the era that followed big game hunting was marked by a desperate search for food. It was believed that people were constantly on the move, driven by hunger, made miserable by exposure, and desperate for their safety in a hostile environment.

This may have been the situation in some regions, but it definitely was not the case in the Illinois River Valley. At horizon eleven, the people had already domesticated the dog, learned the art of basket making, and were probably good wood workers. Stone tools include both flaked points and smooth adzes made by grinding and polishing. The adzes were very likely used to make dugout canoes and trim posts for houses. The stone slabs used to grind seeds made flour that was probably used for both bread and porridge. The people also gathered nuts, dug clams, caught fish, and hunted deer and other game.

Professor Struever was struck by the variety of foods collected. He concluded that here, in 6400 B.C., without any knowledge of nutrition, people were enjoying a diet that could not have been improved upon by a modern nutritionist.

House floors and post holes have been identified at horizon eleven indicating that the people probably lived in permanent houses, but the community covered no more than three-quarters of an acre. It is possible that the little village was not occupied year-round. The people may have moved to spring or summer camps in the high country, but the village was the main home for the people.

Best evidence for permanence are burials in a designated cemetery, perhaps the oldest cemetery yet discovered in North America. Red ocher was spread on the bodies and flat stones or logs were placed over each grave. Grave offerings included stone knives, hammerstones, and other tools. One grave contained a tortoise shell bowl and a bone awl. The graves, however, show little class distinction.

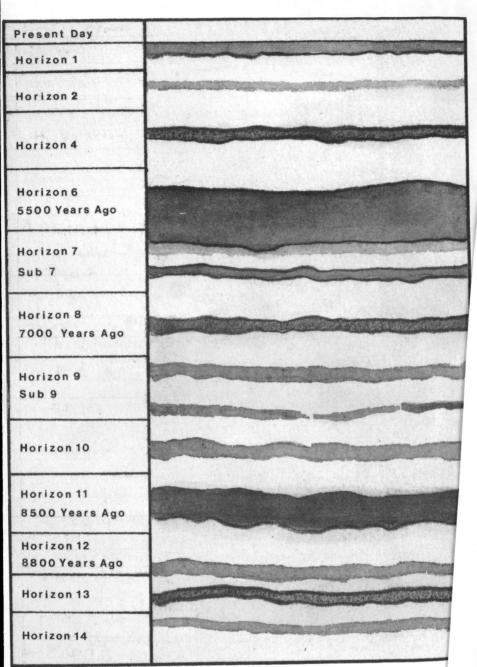

Present Day	
Horizon 1	
Horizon 2	
Horizon 4	
Horizon 6 5500 Years Ago	
Horizon 7 Sub 7	
Horizon 8 7000 Years Ago	
Horizon 9 Sub 9	
Horizon 10	
Horizon 11 8500 Years Ago	
Horizon 12 8800 Years Ago	
Horizon 13	
Horizon 14	

Dark strata mark levels of human occupation at Koster that date back more than 8,800 years. Workers at the site call the levels horizons of occupation.

For some reason, secondary burials were the common practice. The bodies apparently were left uncovered until decay began. Only then was the burial completed. The practice, also followed by the Red Paint People of Port au Choix, may have been the carry-over of an Arctic tradition established when ancestors of these people lived in a region of frozen winter ground.

Dogs were also buried in ceremonial graves with stone slabs or logs serving as markers and protection from animals. The dogs, with large heads and rather small bodies, were probably used to track game.

The next level up, some thirty feet below the surface and eight thousand years old, is not as rich in relics, which suggests a short-term occupancy. The relics that have been found, however, show little change in life style.

We must move up to horizon eight, twenty-one feet below the surface and some seven thousand years old, to find significant change. Here a new style of house building was developed. The homes were set in rows of terraces on the sloping valley floor. The location gave better drainage and protection from spring floods, and cutting the house floors into terraces allowed packed earth to serve as the lower portion of the back and sides of the house. The upper parts of the walls were built up with woven sticks supported by vertical posts. The walls were plastered with mud and then the house was roofed over with thatch or bark.

Although evidence is too scant from horizon eleven to be certain of the method of building houses, they too were probably made of mud-dabbed sticks. The terracing shown at level eight, however, represents a definite change. We also see an increase of population with the village growing to cover one-and-a-half acres.

Another major change is seen in the appearance of

more varied woodworking tools. Polished stone axes, deeply grooved for hafting to a stout handle, were sturdy enough to allow the men to cut down large trees. The people, thus, had acquired a forest-clearing technology.

Refuse heaps show a marked increase in dependence on hickory nuts harvested from trees that grew on the bluffs above the village. Thus, with closer orientation to the forests, both for timber and for nuts, the people at this horizon had begun to enlarge their resources.

This enlarging trend continued until we see in horizon six, a thick layer of occupation extending from five to ten feet below the surface, that the people had achieved a remarkable diversity. Relics from horizon six show that five thousand eight hundred years ago people were using throwing nets to trap ducks. They had also developed a new technique employing nets, traps, or perhaps special baskets to take fish by the thousands. Tiny schooling fish no more than an inch long were apparently an important harvest. In one refuse deposit, three inches deep and covering six square feet, experts counted the remains of twenty-two thousand of these small fish.

Cooking was done in pits that were lined with clay and then buried under hot coals to fire the clay. Koster archeologists' cite these pits as the budding of the potter's art, but full-scale pottery did not bloom at Koster until much later, and then it arrived some five hundred years after it appeared in many other Archaic regions.

Horizon six, however, does show a surge in artistic expression. Delicate patterns were carved in bone hairpins, and one craftsman made a bone whistle. Stones, drilled to fit on a shaft or pole, were shaped into symmetrical cylinders or disks and polished to a high gloss. These banner stones, as they are called, evidently served as symbols of status.

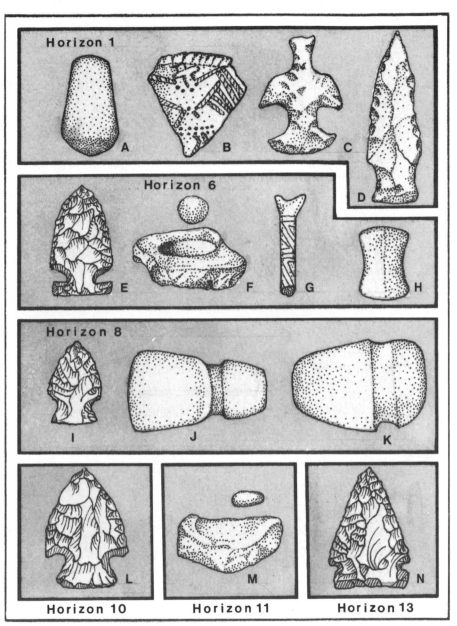

Koster artifacts typical of six different horizons are (A) a polished stone axe, (B) a piece of pottery with a thunderbird design, (C) a bird effigy chipped from stone, (D) a slightly notched point, (E) a deeply notched point, (F) a mortar and grinding stone, (G) the engraved head of a hairpin, (H) a banner stone, probably a symbol of status, (I) a wide point, (J) an adze, (K) an axe, (L) a deeply notched, broad point, (M) a slab mortar and grinding stone, and (N) a delicately notched point.

Some ornaments were used in trade. Copper ore was thus obtained from the Lake Superior deposits mined by the Old Copper People. At Koster, this copper was fashioned into beads, and these were traded in turn to obtain a high quality flint from the Ohio River Valley. Craftsmen continued to make both tools and ornaments that served as grave offerings, and burials for the dead of horizon six were more elaborate and apparently more ritualistic than before. The cemetery was located well away from the village. The village itself had grown to cover five acres with a population perhaps six to seven times greater than the population of the settlement of horizon eleven.

One of the most fascinating developments at horizon six, however, is an increased dependence on seed foods, particularly from flood plain plants such as lambs-quarter and marsh elder. In later years, evidence from Koster and nearby related sites shows that the people began to experiment with marsh elder, because both the quality and quantity of seeds from this cranberry-like shrub improved. Though still growing in a wild state, the plant was evidently cultivated. Perhaps ditches were even dug to run water to the healthiest plants. Thus, a kind of farming began almost two thousand years before full-scale crop farming was introduced to the Illinois River Valley.

Evidence of this advance is found in horizon four, four feet below the surface with an age of almost three thousand years. This level is marked by a shift in climate. The weather turned cold and wet, and the change brought an improvement in the upland vegetation. The people took advantage of the improvement, harvesting more hickory and hazel nuts, pecans, and acorns from the forest and increasing the take of deer, turkeys, racoons, and other upland game. Grave offerings, following a steady trend, grew more elaborate, but the population of Koster remained the same. The big change was still to come.

And come it did, a revolution in the Koster way of life brought about by the introduction of crop farming. Relics uncovered just one to two feet below the surface, and dated from a thousand to sixteen hundred years ago, show that the crops included corn, beans, and squash. A clamshell with a hole punched out for a wooden handle served as a hoe. Deep pits were dug and lined as storage bins, and large cauldrons of fired clay, the first real Koster pottery, served as cooking vessels.

Thanks to the appearance of the bow and arrow, hunters increased their efficiency. With crops and a ready supply of game, it is no surprise that populations took a big jump. The village at this level covered twenty-five acres. A more bountiful life gave more leisure time so that craftsmen were able to fashion even more elaborate grave offerings. Effigies of birds and animals were delicately chipped from flint. Pottery was often decorated with religious motifs or totem signs. Evidence of borrowed religion is seen in carvings of a long-nosed god that was worshipped by people on the Gulf Coast far to the south.

The changes at Koster were not all good ones. For the first time skeletons are found with arrow points embedded in rib cages or pelvic areas. Warfare, probably due to the pressure of increased populations throughout the area, had begun at Koster.

We cannot really blame farming for the advent of war, but farming does introduce many new concepts such as ownership of property, rights to water, and organized use of labor. Even today, such concepts lie at the root of many disputes. Certainly farming, with the increased population it allowed, made life more complicated.

How did farming come to the Illinios Valley? Despite the early experimentation with marsh elder, it did not originate at Koster. It most likely was introduced through trade or perhaps by a migrating tribe, and although we cannot be certain of its exact place of origin, it probably came from a land far to the south. That is where we must go to search for the first farmers.

Chapter Eleven

The Search for Corn

After digging and sifting through the dirt of twenty-eight cave floors in Mexico's Tehuacán Valley and finding nothing, Richard S. MacNeish might have been justified in giving up the quest. He already had spent several seasons searching for and exploring caves in Guatemala, Honduras, and Mexico. There had been many disappointments, but he had learned enough, and there had been enough learned by others to convince MacNeish that he had come at last to the right place. The Tehuacán Valley had to solve the puzzle of corn.

The puzzle had long fascinated scientists. When Europeans arrived in the New World, natives from Peru to Canada were cultivating the crop. Even then, there were more than one hundred and fifty domestic varieties of the plant. Today, with many more hybrid varieties, corn is the major crop of the Western Hemisphere and the third most important crop in the world.

Where did it come from? How was it developed? This was the puzzle.

For several years it was the belief of some botanists that corn may have originated through the cross-breeding of two wild grasses, *teosinte* and *tripsacum*. Both these grasses bore seeds in pods, and both gave off pollen from tassles that grew out of the pods.

Even though these wild grasses had features similar to true corn, some genetic experts, including Paul C. Mengelsdorf of Harvard University, searched for a different ancestry. All through the 1940s, Mengelsdorf experimented with various corn-like grasses. He found that *teosinte,* instead of being a parent of corn, probably was

The tripsacum *plant, left, and its seed pods, center, along with* teosinte *pod, right, were once believed to be ancestors of domestic corn, but we now know that these plants have a different place in the corn family.*

created through the accidental crossbreeding between true corn and *tripsacum*. This and other experiments led him to the startling conclusion that the ancestor of corn was corn itself.

Although the ancestral plant no longer existed, Mengelsdorf theorized that it would have been something like a very small popcorn with each kernel enclosed in a pod. Centuries of cross-breeding with other grasses, including *teosinte* and *tripsacum,* Mengelsdorf said, could have produced the many varieties of corn that were found under cultivation by European explorers in the New World.

Mengelsdorf's theory gradually gained support from the field work of both botanists and archeologists. Significant support first came from drill cores taken from dry lake flats near Mexico City in 1953. Corn pollen was found in cores taken from strata that were estimated to be eighty thousand years old. Because it predated the advent of farming in any form, the pollen had to come from wild corn.

Meanwhile, Herbert Dick, one of Mengelsdorf's students, found tiny corncobs deep in the floor of Bat Cave, New Mexico. MacNeish soon made similar discoveries in La Perra Cave not far from Mexico's Gulf Coast. The cobs seemed to fit the ancestral corn that Mengelsdorf envisioned, and age of the cobs was set at four to five thousand years. Here, it seemed, was the earliest evidence of the domestic plant.

Hoping to find even earlier evidence, MacNeish continued searching caves in northeastern Mexico. The dry soil in the caves preserved corncobs well, and he found more evidence of domestic plants, but none older than five thousand years. In 1958, he shifted his attention to caves in Honduras and Guatemala. It was a disappointing season, producing no useful evidence. So, in 1959, he came back to Mexico, searching in Chiapas, the southernmost state. He found no corncobs, but the earth in one cave yielded corn pollen that was again five thousand years old.

Now, having searched both north and south of the central Mexican highlands, MacNeish reasoned that he should focus his attention on this region. Mengelsdorf believed that ancestral corn probably originated in high country, and this made Mexico's highlands look all the more promising. The first caves in the region that Mac-Neish explored, however, were in the State of Oaxaca at the southern end of the highlands. The caves yielded no traces of early corn, so MacNeish moved farther north to the Tehuacán Valley not far from the city of Puebla.

For a time, it appeared that the search here would also prove fruitless, but on February 21, 1960, while digging in their twenty-ninth cave, MacNeish and his helpers found six cobs of early domestic corn. To MacNeish, three of the cobs seemed older than any he had seen before.

Carbon 14 dating showed that the three cobs were five thousand six hundred years old. They were, indeed, the oldest domestic corncobs ever recovered.

Believing that farming probably had its origins in several different regions, MacNeish did not claim that the Tehuacán Valley was the home of the first farmers of the New World. He did claim that the place deserved extensive exploration by a team of specialists.

His fellow scientists agreed. In the months that followed MacNeish's discovery, the National Science Foundation, the Peabody Foundation for Archeology, and the Agricultural Branch of the Rockefeller Foundation based in Mexico City, all gave their support for a full scale expedition. Geologists, botanists, soil experts, and of course, archeologists, were enlisted from many different universities across Mexico and the United States. The scientific crew alone eventually totaled fifty men and women.

Work began in the summer of 1961, and long before this first season ended, it was clear that the Tehuacán Valley not only held evidence of corn's evolution, but also held the much broader stories of the development of farming in general, of crafts, such as, weaving and pottery, of engineering, of politics and government, and of religion. Expanded and extended, the expedition continued through 1964. Twelve different sites were excavated. More than a million separate relics and other finds gave evidence of human occupations stretching back through twelve thousand years. A thousand animal bones, including those of extinct antelopes and horses, were unearthed and identified.

Remains of more than eighty thousand plants, including twenty-five thousand specimens of corn, were discovered. Included among the latter finds were tiny corncobs little more than half an inch long. These proved to be seven thousand years old, and botanists agreed that the cobs came from the very plant that Mengelsdorf's theoretical genius had envisioned back in the 1940s—wild, ancestral corn that no one had ever seen before.

All the finds gave a record of continuous occupation that was truly remarkable. The floor of one cave alone was built up of twenty-eight levels of occupation with the bottom level revealing an age of eight thousand years.

Although farming may have had separate origins in other regions, the Tehuacán Valley presents a full record of how it evolved there. It is a fascinating record.

From about 10,000 to 7000 B.C. the valley supported a small population of people who hunted jackrabbits, turtles, rats, birds, and other small animals. Rarely, they were able to kill one of the larger almost-extinct animals such as a horse or antelope. Although they gathered seeds and fruits from wild plants, they made no advances toward farming.

Tools were made of flaked stone, crudely shaped for scraping or carving. The finest projectile points were leaf-shaped. Cruder ones were triangular with a flat base. The archeologist named this first phase Ajuerado.

From about 6700 B.C. to 5000 B.C., during what is called El Riego phase, the people of the valley increased their food gathering activities. A domestic squash and the avocado were grown, but most of the food still came from wild plants, including a wild bean, a wild chili pepper, and the wild amaranth, a relative of the tumbleweed.

In addition to flaked tools, stone choppers and grinding stones appear. The latter include mortars, pestles, and polished pounding stones. El Riego phase also shows the first trend toward more settled living. During the harvest season, several families apparently lived together in a temporary settlement. After the harvest, they broke up again into smaller, nomadic, hunting units. Graves of this period suggest increased burial ritual.

Starting about 5000 B.C., in what has been named the Coxcatlán phase, the number of domesticated plants increased. In addition to amaranth, squash, and chili peppers, the people planted a second variety of squash, the water-bottle gourd, tepary beans, jack beans, probably the common bean, and, for the first time, corn.

Even though corn was finally brought under cultivation in this phase, neither it nor the other domestic crops were of high importance. The Coxcatlán people still relied on gathering, hunting, and trapping for ninety percent of their food. Just the same, some of the people had the spare time to hollow out and shape stones into water bowls and to make larger food grinding instruments with roller-like manos and flat stone metates. Other tools showed little change except that spear points became smaller, better shaped, and some bore barbs near the base.

The Coxcatlán phase lasted until about 3400 B.C. before it gave way in a major change to the Abejas culture. The domestic dog appeared, and the consumption of food from domesticated plants increased from ten to thirty percent. For the first time, people began to live in fixed settlements consisting of several small pit houses.

This culture continued until about 2300 B.C., giving way to the Perrón phase, which was characterized by the manufacture of pottery and the planting for hybridized, improved corn.

The pace of development increased rapidly. The Perrón phase was followed by Ajalpán which soon evolved into the Santa Maria. In about 1500 B.C. pottery became more refined, village life more complex, and religious ceremony more elaborate. It included a figurine cult. The clay figures probably represented family gods.

In about 850 B.C. streams were diverted into ditches that led to fields of corn and other crops. The valley's population increased rapidly. Temple mounds were erected. Less time was needed to obtain food, but a priesthood had control of the people. There was little leisure time. Trade began during the Santa Maria phase. Artifacts show influence from several outside cultures, particularly the Olmec culture centered southeast of the Tehuacán Valley.

By 200 B.C. the Olmec influence declined, replaced largely by the influence of Mount Alban people to the south and west of Tehuacán. During this, the Palo Blanco phase, large irrigation systems developed and hilltop ceremonial centers surrounded by villages appeared. There was also clear evidence of specialization with craftsmen working full time as potters, weavers, or dyers. Salt was mined from natural deposits, adding an important new industry and another trade commodity. New crops included tomatoes, guavas, and peanuts. Wild turkeys were domesticated.

The Palo Blanco phase continued until 700 A.D. when it was replaced by the Venta Salada phase, which was marked by another shift in outside influence, this time to the Mixtecs north of the valley. True cities appeared. There was a standing army, a complex religion, and expanded trade. By now, farmers produced eighty-five percent of the food.

This phase continued until the time of the Spanish conquest. The only change was a shift in outside influence to the Aztecs in the Valley of Mexico.

Farming techniques, seeds, and perhaps some plants spread through trade. Trade undoubtedly hastened development, but even so, the development was generally slow. MacNeish concludes that farming rose in the valley, not as a revolution, but as an evolution.

The evolution of farming in Tehuacán provides a significant contrast with what we know of the evolution of farming in the Old World. It is believed that Old World farming first began in the highlands of the Middle East where villages, pottery, and population increases developed much earlier than they did in the New World chronology. New World farmers domesticated far more plants and far fewer animals than did Old World farmers. The only crops the two hemispheres had in common at the time of Columbus were the yam, the water bottle gourd, and cotton. Unique to the New World were white and sweet potatoes, vanilla, two varieties of chili, chives, panic grass, amaranth, sunflower, chocolate, peanuts, manioc, oca, pumpkin, three species of squash, five species of beans, and of course, corn.

Tame dogs and beekeeping appeared early in both the Old and the New World, but the only other animals domesticated in the New World were the turkey, the guinea pig, and three relatives of the camel, the llama, alpaca, and the vicuna. There were no herds of sheep, cattle, or hogs, no flocks of hens or geese. New World farmers continued to rely on hunting and trapping as the main source of meat, fur, and hides.

These differences, and the very gradual evolution in the New World of farming argue against introduction of agriculture from the Old World by pre-Columbus visits. As we shall see in a later chapter, there are several arguments in support of such visits. But if farming had been brought to the New World from across the seas, it would have brought an abrupt change. And no such change occurred in the Tehuacán Valley, one of the oldest farming centers yet discovered.

Chapter Twelve

The City-State

In 1519, when Hernando Cortez and his small army arrived in the Valley of Mexico, they stared in disbelief at the Aztec capital, a city of shining buildings and temples that rose as a citadel in the middle of a shallow lake. The sight was totally unexpected. Here was a match for any city of the Old World. This prize of conquest was surely the capital of a new civilization. At least, it seemed new to the Spaniards.

Actually, the Aztecs had modeled their city after a much older, much greater capital that had fallen to ruin just twenty-five miles to the north. It was called Teotihuacán.

For more than five hundred years, Teotihuacán had dominated the politics, economy, trade, art, and religions of Central America. At the peak of its power around 500 A.D., the city was larger than ancient Rome, and its biggest temple, the flat-topped Pyramid of the Sun, had a larger base than Egypt's great pyramid of Cheops.

Despite the city's fall, its temples retained their mysterious power. At the time of the conquest, Indians still wor-

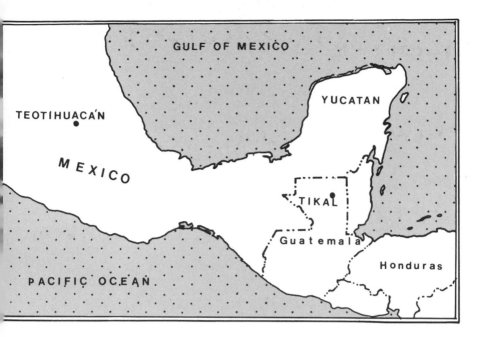

shipped at Teotihuacán, and they would continue to worship there for many years to come. Even as ruins, the Pyramid of the Sun, the Pyramid of the Moon, and the broad avenue that linked the two monuments, known as the Street of the Dead, remained important landmarks to the natives.

Teotihuacán was built on a well-designed plan of cross streets that formed a grid of equal blocks just like those of a modern city. A river had even been diverted so that its flow would conform with the street alignment. The river water apparently was not fit to drink because canals had been built to bring spring water to the city from the nearby mountains. There was also an efficient drainage system with many ditches that rapidly carried off storm and waste water.

The city's planners had even set aside special districts for various crafts. Thus potters, leather workers, dyers, weavers, and stone workers each had their own districts. There were even foreign quarters for those not native to the area.

The arts were encouraged. Stone carvings and murals

decorated temples and public buildings, and clay pots and figurines, many of them mass produced from molds, were important trade goods.

Cortez and his men were not interested in ruins, and with few exceptions, the travelers who came later and did take an interest were not impressed by the rubble. Indeed, our own century had dawned before archeologists began to appreciate the full significance of Teotihuacán. Now after many years of digging, restoration, and study, they can say at last that here stood the first urban center ever built in the New World.

True, there are many older ruins in Peru, Yucatán, and Mexico, but they all mark the sites of religious centers. Most had just a few dwellings to house the resident priests and their families. Market days were held regularly at many of these temple cities, but they were not true commercial centers.

Teotihuacán, originally built under influence of the Omecs, whose culture spread inland from the Gulf Coast, probably began as a temple city. For a long time, it apparently was populated only by the priesthood. Then, about the time of Christ, the city began to grow rapidly.

Several factors contributed to this rapid growth. Of chief importance was trade. The city stood in a narrow valley that led from the vast Valley of Mexico to the Valley of Pueblo to the southeast. The Valley of Pueblo led in turn to the Gulf Coast and on to Yucatán.

Another factor was obsidian. The hills near the city held abundant deposits of this raw material for tools, weapons, and ornaments. Both worked and unworked stone brought wealth to the city's tradesmen. Later, when a deposit of higher quality obsidian was developed twenty miles northeast of the city, Teotihuacán retained full control of the trade.

Another factor was water. Springs in the hills provided a steady supply both for the city dwellers and for the farmers who fed the growing population. Rainfall in the Mexican highlands is sporadic, but even long spells of dry weather did not reduce the vital supply of water.

Recent evidence suggests that farmers of Teotihuacán may have invented the highly productive technique of water gardening on small artificial islands or *chinampas.* Such islands seem to have been built in a swampy region of the city. Centuries later, water gardening was still practiced by the Aztecs and their neighbors on the shores of the lake that surrounded their city. Indeed, the *chinampas* survive today as the Floating Gardens of Zochimilco, a major tourist attraction in Mexico City. The technique, if it did indeed originate at Teotihuacán, would have been yet another factor encouraging growth.

As the city grew, so did the strength of its trade. Craftsmen were drawn to Teotihuacán, where they could work together, exchange ideas, and improve their workmanship and their tools. Unique styles that served as a trademark for quality soon developed, and this not only contributed to further growth of the city but also broadened its influence.

Religion, however, played the major role in the city's reaching power. Even though Teotihuacán had become a business capital, it retained its religious origins. It was a mecca for pilgrims, who arrived by the thousands both to worship and to spend their money on food, lodging, and trade goods. Indeed, we can say that the tourist business was brisk for the city's merchants.

Awesome evidence of the city's religious zeal is provided by the two great pyramids. Between 100 and 200 A.D., the era of peak building activity, the Pyramid of the Sun was raised on the east side of the Street of the Dead.

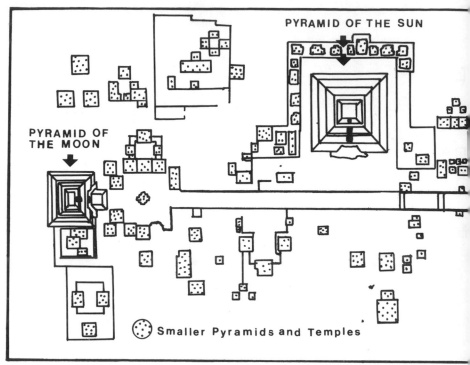

PYRAMID OF THE SUN

PYRAMID OF
THE MOON

Smaller Pyramids and Temples

*Central structures, including the Pyramid of the Moon to the
north, the Pyramid of the Sun, and the two great plazas
dominated Teotihuacan.*

Built on the site of an older temple, the pyramid has an
earth-fill core and is faced with rock. Each side of its square
base measures 689 feet—more than twice the length of a
football field. The monument rises 210 feet to its platform
top.

Later, at the north end of the Street of the Dead, the
Pyramid of the Moon was built in same earth-core, rock-
facing manner. Though smaller than the first structure,
the Pyramid of the Moon is still impressive. Its square base
measures 490 feet on each side, and it is 150 feet high.

Today's tourists to Teotihuacán have to remind
themselves that these massive structures were built without
machinery. The only "earthmovers" available were men
and women with baskets.

Large as the two pyramids are, they may not have
been the chief temples of worship. Small temples lined

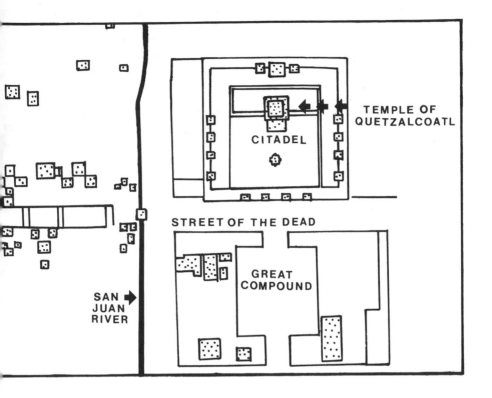

STREET OF THE DEAD

TEMPLE OF QUETZALCOATL

CITADEL

GREAT COMPOUND

SAN JUAN RIVER

both sides of the Street of the Dead, and south of the Pyramid of the Sun was a large plaza enclosed by rectangular buildings and, on the east side, another temple. It was carved with figures of the feathered serpent, an ancient deity of Mexico that was worshipped by the Aztecs as the god Quetzalcoatl. Thus, archeologists named the structure the Temple of Quetzalcoatl even though the people of Teotihuacán may have known the god by another name. The plaza itself, which has been named the Citadel, apparently was used for religious festivals that were officiated over by priests who occupied the rectangular buildings that bordered the plaza.

To the west, directly across the street from the Citadel, a second large plaza was enclosed by buildings that were probably used by government officials as homes and offices. This plaza, called the Great Compound, served as a marketplace and political center.

Early in the study of Teotihuacán's ruins, it was

thought that the Street of the Dead with its plazas, pyramids, and smaller temples was simply the remains of another temple city. Today, however, we know that the street was the main avenue of a city that spread over eight square miles. The grid of the city lined up precisely with the north-south axis of the Street of the Dead. Even streets two miles away from the main avenue were parallel or at right angles to it.

René Millon of the University of Rochester who led recent excavations that revealed the full extent of the city, found that Teotihuacán surveyors used bench marks to guide them in laying out the grid. Carved in bedrock or scratched on the clay floors of houses, the marks are circles bisected by crossing quadrant lines. The marks made it possible to maintain the grid pattern even over hilly terrain.

The grid pattern allowed easy division of the city into districts for the various craft workers, and it was necessary for orderly growth. Millon has estimated that Teotihuacán, at its peak, reached a population of at least fifty thousand, but this is conservative. The total, according to Millon, might have reached a hundred thousand. To this must be added a transient population of pilgrims and tradesmen who numbered in the thousands during religious festivals.

Early in the history of the city, farmers lived in the country on the land they cultivated, but as the city grew, the farmers and their families moved into a district of their own inside the city limits. This move toward centralization can be traced all through the Valley of Mexico and neighboring regions. Farmers living in remote areas gathered in small settlements patterned after the big city.

We do not know what caused this centralization, but the motive must have been great because it meant that the farmer had to commute daily to his fields. There may have been raiding bands that made isolated country living dangerous. It is also possible the community living with easy access to religious ceremony, trade goods, art and entertainment, and the latest gossip of the day was an attraction that could not be denied.

The typical dwelling of Teotihuacán was a single-story apartment building. Millon found that the buildings had square floor plans with each side of the square measuring sixty-two feet. From one building to the next, the measurement varied rarely and then only by a few inches.

The outer walls of the square were bare and windowless, presenting a solid barrier to the street for protection and privacy. Inside, however, the small rooms were arranged around roofless patios, which not only gave open space and light but also provided a sunny gathering space. When it rained, the roofs drained into the patios, which had ditches that led to the central drainage systems.

Volcanic rock, abundant in the area, provided the basic building material. The rock was crushed and then mixed with earth, lime, and water to form a hard-drying, moisture-resistant plaster. This plaster was used to build foundations and floors. It was also spread on the walls, which were built up of rock or adobe, and it was used to cover the roof lattice of timbers and sticks.

Thus, the homes were built to last. Even so, Millon found evidence in several sections of urban renewal, where old houses had been torn down and replaced by new structures. Such renewal projects would not be possible without the authority of a strong central government. With good engineering, durable construction, and strong central authority, it is little wonder that Teotihuacán lasted through the centuries.

Millon also found remarkable evidence of specialization. Not only was the city divided into districts for various crafts, but the districts themselves were also subdivided according to various skills and methods. For instance, obsidian workers who used a flaking method to shape tools and ornaments lived and worked separately from those who used the core blade technique. In the potters' district, there was a special section for workers who mass produced a common cooking pot with the mold method.

It is easy to imagine that the crafts were controlled by a highly organized system of guilds, with the guilds in turn controlled by the government. Work may have been inspected regularly to make sure that quality was maintained. It seems likely that production was spurred on by a quota system.

Teotihuacán reached its peak population in about 500 A.D. It was at this time that many of the urban renewal projects were undertaken, and this suggests that the city's government may have attained its greatest strength. We do know that the city now had a standing army. Soldiers were available to enforce laws, see that objections were put down, and be sure that projects, such as urban renewal, were carried out.

Apparently, soldiers were also used to maintain control in distant territory. Military influence reached as far as Mayan cities in Guatemala. Embassies were staffed in these cities with Teotihuacán soldiers and priests. During Teotihuacán rule, Tikal, the major Mayan city, changed from a temple city to an urban center with a population of some ten thousand.

Although soldiers were posted in distant cities, it appears that Teotihuacán power did not grow out of force or conquest. In fact, the five hundred years of Teotihuacán dominance were remarkably peaceful. This may have caused the city's downfall.

We do not really know what caused the collapse, but one suggestion is that rebelling tribes from the north overran the city. After centuries of peace, the government and its soldiers were ill-prepared for warfare. There were no walls, no formal defenses of any kind to protect against invaders. Support for the suggestion of an invasion comes mainly from the record of fire and looting, which occurred in about 750 A.D. By this time, however, Teotihuacán influence had already started to decline.

The decline actually began several years before the fire. The quality of pottery and other goods produced for trade had dropped, building had turned shoddy, and the population itself had begun to shrink. This suggests decay from within. Perhaps, the government had become top-heavy and corrupt, and the people had learned to resist authority. The looting and fire may have been the culmination of revolt.

There is also evidence of climatic change in the Valley of Mexico, which coincided with the decline of Teotihuacán. A drying trend perhaps at last reduced the water supply. Crop production then would have dropped. When farmers could no longer support the large population, people would move away in search of better lands, or at least lands where the population pressure was not so great. Such a shift would have left the city ripe for either conquest or rebellion.

Though we do not know exactly what caused the collapse, we do know that it had repercussions throughout Central America. Soon after Teotihuacán's fall, the Mayans began to abandon many of their temple cities. In southern Mexico, Monte Alban, an important religious and cultural center, was also abandoned.

How far did the Teotihuacán realm extend? We cannot say, but it is possible that a culture that flourished for some thirteen centuries in the desert of what is now Arizona may have once been within the Teotihuacán sphere.

The desert culture is known today as Hohokam, a Puma Indian word that means "people who have vanished." Mystery still surrounds these people, but evidence of Mexican influence is unmistakable.

Like the people of Teotihuacán, the Hohokam people were builders. Their flat-topped pyramids and their ball courts match the ruins of Central Mexico. Hohokam clay figurines are almost exactly like figurines made by Mexican craftsmen. Hohokam farmers grew corn and other crops imported from Mexico. They even obtained rubber for the ball used in their court game from the jungles of Mexico.

The greatest Hohokam achievement was the construction of dams and canals for the irrigation of their crops. Some of these canals were thirty feet wide and twenty-five miles long. They made up the largest irrigation system ever built by prehistoric man in the New World.

Hohokam people did not practice class distinction or engage in war. They lived peacefully, side-by-side with people of other desert cultures.

It is speculating to put Hohokam people within the Teotihuacán realm, and it would be a wild flight of fancy to suggest that this early Arizonan culture was established by a tribe that migrated from the Valley of Mexico. Thus, with no evidence to the contrary, there is room to wonder.

Unfortunately, Hohokam dates are uncertain. The culture may have started as early as 300 B.C. or as late as 300 A.D. We do know that around 1100 A.D., after a drop in rainfall, the Hohokam way of life vanished. This was long after Teotihuacán's fall.

In Central Mexico, the small urban centers established during Teotihuacán times continued to exist as separate political units well after the fall of the great city. Around 900 A.D. Central America was united under the Toltec empire, but after two centuries, Mexico was again reduced to separate states, not to be reunited once more until the Aztec conquest began about 1400 A.D.

The Aztecs were still adding to their realm when Cortez led his small band of gold-hungry adventurers into the Valley of Mexico. Thus, the great city-state empires first achieved by Teotihuacán were never seen in Central America again.

Chapter Thirteen

The Mound Builders

The largest earthen structure ever raised by prehistoric man stands today behind a forest of neon signs and a wall of motels, super markets, restaurants, and gas stations. Motorists speeding along Interstate 55 in southern Illinois can still see the top of Monks Mound. After all, it covers fourteen acres and rises a hundred feet above the plain, but the base of the mound is hidden behind the clutter of civilization. For the average American, the significance of Monks Mound is almost totally lost to view.

Here was the capital of a complex culture that dominated the eastern heartland of North America for six centuries. Here was the final expression of a tradition that can be traced back to the Red Paint People and the Old Copper Culture. And here freeway construction and commercial development have destroyed forty percent of the archeological record.

Sad to say, the abuse given the Monks Mound site is typical. Mound sites throughout the Mississippi Basin and along the eastern seaboard have suffered years of abuse. During most of the last century, the sites were looted by commercial relic hunters who made little note of what they found or where they sold it. And ever since Europeans arrived in the New World, the mounds have been the subject of ill-founded, often ridiculous theories. With so much of the record lost, it was hard to disprove these theories.

Most of them were based on the prejudice that the American Indian was too primitive, too lazy, and too stupid to build anything more ambitious than a tepee or crude hut. The mounds, the theories said, had to be built by someone else—a vanished race. And who were these people? Here's where the guesswork really turned wild. Some said the mounds were the work of early Norsemen. Others argued that Phoenicians, Egyptians, Medieval Irish monks, or Welshmen built the mounds; anybody but the Indian.

The prejudice against the Indian was based in large part on the terrible toll of diseases brought to the New World by European explorers. With little resistance to small pox, pneumonia, and other maladies, epidemics swept through tribe after tribe. In many cases, Indian populations fell so drastically that the survivors were reduced in just a few years to a pitiful existence. No longer were they able to follow the old traditions or maintain crafts or skills that had given them pride and dignity. White settlers, arriving in the wake of epidemics, thus saw little evidence of greatness among these native Americans.

Thanks to the work of hundreds of dedicated archeologists, however, we can now tell the story of the mounds with some confidence. True, many gaps in the record, many puzzles remain, but we know that the mounds were, in fact, built by ancestors of the Indians. There was no "vanished race." We also know that mound building was just one facet of a religious cult, and that the cult was not limited to a single culture but spread across many different cultures, many different language groups. The cult was complex, and through the years it went through many variations.

Another facet of the cult was trade for funeral goods. We have already seen that the Red Paint People of Port au Choix made grave offerings. By about 4000 B.C. these people began trading with their neighbors in order to obtain even better material for their burials. A similar trade began among the people of the Old Copper Culture on the northern shores of the Great Lakes in about 3000 B.C.

The origins of mound building itself, however, are still shrouded in mystery. The Red Paint People sometimes used natural mounds of earth or gravel for their burials, but they did not build artificial mounds. The earliest known artificial mounds, built about 1500 B.C., are among the largest and most complex yet discovered. They were not built primarily for burials. Obviously, there is a gap in the record.

These early mounds are in Louisiana at a site called Poverty Point. Here, recent aerial photography revealed a series of six concentric octagons flanked by two mounds, a large one to the west and a smaller one to the north. All were built on a vast scale.

The largest octagon has a diameter of almost a mile— 1,422 yards, to be exact. The smallest, inner octagon is 545 yards across. The octagons are built up of ridges two yards high. To the west, a ramp leads up to the bigger mound. It is 218 yards long and twenty-two yards high.

We do not know exactly what purpose the mounds

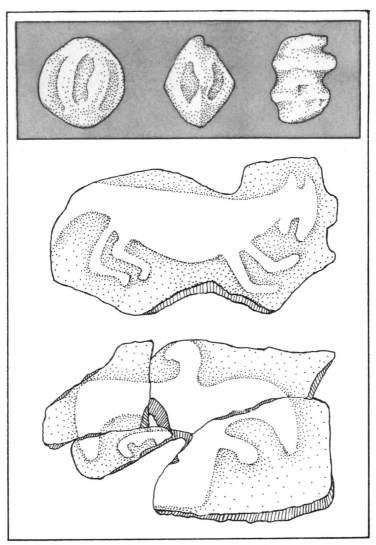

*Clay balls (top) found at Poverty Point were heated and
dropped in pots to cook food. The pots were decorated with
highly stylized beasts and birds.*

served, but the people who built them may have been sun worshippers. On the first day of spring and the first day of fall—the equinoxes—when night and day have the same length, a person standing on the western mound can see the sun rise directly over the center of the octagons.

People lived at Poverty Point with some permanence. The most common artifact is a clay ball, which was heated, and then dropped in a cooking pot. Thousands of these cooking balls have been collected.

Other artifacts unearthed at the site include small effigies of birds and clay figurines. The clay replicas of humans bear a striking resemblance to clay figures produced by the Olmecs, the culture that had begun to flourish in the Gulf Coast of Mexico well before 1500 B.C.

The resemblance has led several archeologists to believe that the mound building was introduced to North America through Olmec influence. It is true that the Olmecs were builders, and they did indeed have an influence on Teotihuacán and in the Valley of Tehuacán. Olmecs, however, covered their pyramids with clay and built mosaic pavement with a pattern of curving blocks. In addition to figurines, Olmec artists also depicted a cat-like god in stone and clay, and they carved huge chunks of basalt into human heads. None of these features of their culture appear at Poverty Point.

The Olmecs, furthermore, were farmers. Their civilization, in fact, was the first to be based on a farming economy in the New World. If their influence did extend as far north as Poverty Point, it is hard to explain why the mound builders there lived as hunters and gatherers. It seems unlikely that they would have adopted Olmec figurines and mound building, but not farming.

Farming did spread through North America from Mexico, but that did not begin to happen until about 1000

B.C., five hundred years after the mounds at Poverty Point were built. Even if the Olmecs did influence the earthworks at Poverty Point, no evidence has yet been found of similar constructions elsewhere. Poverty Point is unique. Thus, it does not represent a wide-spread cult of mound builders. So the Olmec origin for mound building remains highly debatable.

The first mound builders who did represent a widespread cult have been named Adena after a well-known site near Adena, Ohio. The cult emerged between 1000 and 800 B.C. at a time when farming was gradually being adopted and crude pottery was being made. Apparently originating in Ohio, the cult spread into Indiana, Kentucky, West Virginia, and Pennsylvania. More than 200 Adena sites have been identified.

Although the people practicing the Adena cult cultivated sunflower, goosefoot, marsh elder, pigweed, squash, and corn, they still relied on hunting and gathering for most of their food. They had no cities. The typical community rarely consisted of more than five or six houses framed upon circles of posts. Since they were still devoting most of their time to hunting and gathering, it is remarkable that these people could spare the time and energy for mound building. And with their small communities, it is just as remarkable that they could organize the manpower required for such prodigious undertakings.

Followers of the cult built both burial mounds and worship mounds. The latter, called sacred circles, were ridges of earth usually more than a hundred yards in diameter. Gaps in the ridges served as gateways into the circle. At some sites, two or more circles were linked to form larger enclosures.

Because of class distinctions, burial ritual varied. Those of lower class were cremated and buried in simple graves with few or no relics. People of upper class were buried inside log tombs that were covered with mounds that sometimes rose as high as twenty-two feet. The burial mounds, found both outside and inside sacred circles, were sometimes built over post houses. It is not known if these were dwellings or shrines, but they were burned to the ground, apparently as part of the funeral ritual.

Bodies were placed in the tomb face up and in a fully extended position. They were covered with ocher or whatever other natural red pigment was available. In some cases, it appears that a tomb was left open, available for a second interment. In other cases, the dead were buried with a skull, which could have been the severed head of human sacrifice, a trophy of war, or the honored remains of a relative.

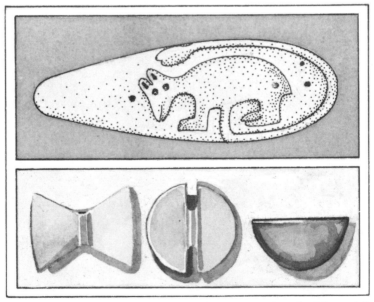

Adena artifacts include banner stones (bottom) and tablets with carvings, used either for relief printing on cloth or to hold tatooing pigments.

Polished stone gorgets, or ornamental collars, coved at both ends so that they resemble the letter H, and tablets, carved to depict birds and animals in abstact design, were the most common Adena grave offerings. The gorgets were probably worn as ornaments, but some of them have large holes in their centers, which suggest that they may have served as weights for spears. The tablets with their relief carvings could have been used to print dyes on cloth or in tattooing. Bone awls sharp enough to prick a design into skin were often placed beside a tablet.

Smoking pipes, some carved to depict humans or animals, give the earliest evidence of tobacco north of Mexico. Tobacco, which originated in South America, traveled north either through Mexico or the West Indies. Adena smokers probably mixed the dried leaves of local plants with the tobacco.

Native copper, which came through trade from the shores of Lake Superior, was hammered into bracelets, beads, and gorgets. In the graves, the copper decomposed into salts that preserved fragments of cloth. From this accident of chemistry, we know that the mound builders were accomplished weavers, able to make garments of good enough quality to serve as grave offerings. Adena pottery was evidently deemed too crude to be worthy of the dead. It was never placed in a grave.

The Adena cult required trade, and it was through trade that the cult spread. The network of Adena trade is as remarkable as the mounds. It eventually extended into New York State and to the shores of Chesapeake Bay. It spanned different language groups. It overcame suspicion and, perhaps, hostility. The trade was probably achieved through a formal tradition of gift-giving that survived among American Indians into Colonial times. Even in alien territory, a gift-giver won immediate respect and hospitality under this tradition, and the exchange of gifts was the first step in negotiating a treaty or a trade agreement.

A new cult, obviously inspired by Adena practices, appeared in southern Illinois about 300 B.C. It called for bigger mounds and much more lavish funeral offerings.

Named Hopewell for a farm in Ohio where some of its mounds were built, the new cult existed side-by-side with Adena for many years. Then about 100 B.C., Hopewell practices spread from Illinois into Ohio, and by 300 A.D. the new cult had replaced Adena entirely.

The sacred circles were larger and more varied than those of Adena. Rectangles and octagons as well as circles, some more than five hundred yards across, were raised, and they were often linked together to enclose large areas. Burials were almost always within the enclosures.

The burial mounds were usually built in two stages. The first stage was a low mound covering a log tomb containing bodies or shallow pits containing cremated remains. The second stage called for a thick covering of earth that left a mound sometimes thirty-nine feet high and ninety feet wide.

These mounds, and many that were even larger, sometimes contained hundreds of bodies accumulated over several decades. Smaller mounds, containing a single body and many grave goods, marked a burial of an important person.

One individual of high status was buried with 297 pounds of imported obsidian, more than half of the total store of this kind of obsidian collected from all Hopewell sites.

Hopewell artists produced work of great variety and extremely high quality. Copper was shaped into ear spools, beads, gorgets, smoking pipes, axes, adzes, awls, and flat sheets. Thin copper sheets, cut to various designs, were

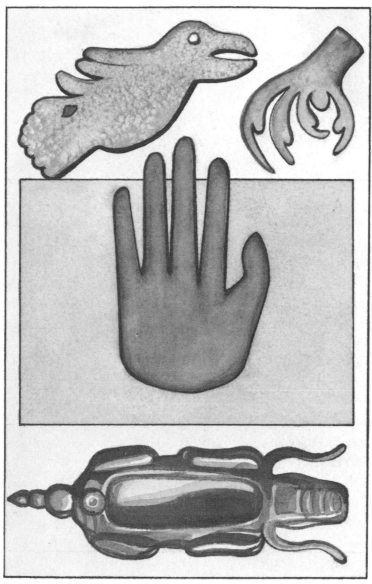

Hopewell funeral offerings include birds cut from flattened copper, bird claws and hands cut from mica, and a symbolic beast carved from stone.

often engraved or embossed. Thick sheets of copper were molded to form breastplates for the body of the deceased. One grave yielded a copper headdress fitted with deer antlers.

Iron from meteors was sometimes combined with copper. Small amounts of gold, lead, and silver have also been found in Hopewell graves. The silver probably was imported from Ontario.

In addition to elegant knives and spearpoints, stone workers made smoking pipes that were often carved to depict bears, birds, frogs, or human heads. One figurine was carved from the ivory of an extinct mammoth.

Hopewell craftsmen were also expert mica workers. Thin sheets of this mineral were cut out and decorated to represent serpents, bird talons, human hands, and human faces. The designs, imaginative and abstract, would be worthy of any museum of modern art.

Potters not only made clay pots for daily use, but also fashioned highly decorated ware for use in burials only. Clay was also used to make smoking pipes, ear spools, and figurines. Cloth fragments, again preseved by copper salts, show that the followers of the Hopewell cult were also excellent weavers.

No distance apparently was too great for Hopewell traders. A special chert with a spotted pattern was imported from North Dakota, or perhaps Montana. A treasured obsidian came from what is now Yellowstone National Park. The tooth of a grizzly bear was probably provided by hunters somewhere in the Rocky Mountains. Turtle shells, conch shells, and the jaws or teeth of sharks, barracudas, and alligators, were imported from the Gulf Coast. These regions were far indeed from Illinois, Indiana, and Ohio, the heart of Hopewell territory, but the people who supplied the trade goods in these distant

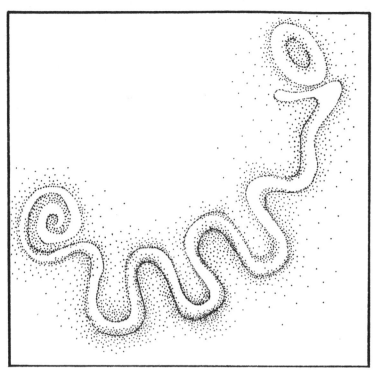

Ohio's serpent mound is the most famous landmark left by the effigy mound builders.

places often adopted Hopewell ways. The distant adoptions did not come about without many variations, but the most unusual variation occurred close to Hopewell heartlands.

This variation took the form of effigy mounds. Large patterns depicting animals and birds were raised in Ohio and Michigan. Perhaps the most famous of these monuments is the Serpent Mound which twists along a ridgetop southwest of Chillicothe, Ohio. The snake is almost 550 yards long. Its tail is coiled and its gaping jaws hold a disklike object represented by a low mound.

The serpent mound apparently did not cover any graves. What purpose did it serve? We don't know. Archeologists are not even sure if effigy mounds were the work of the Hopewell cult, but they were built during the height of the Hopewell era, and thus are considered by most experts as a Hopewell variation.

It was variation of the basic tradition, perhaps that led in about 650 A.D. to the Hopewell decline. Other suggested causes for decline include a change in climate, which made it impossible to grow the breed of corn that Hopewell people depended upon, over-population which forced people to disperse, and excessive demand for grave goods which led to a breakdown in trade.

Although trade did collapse, mound building continued with effigy mound building flourishing in Minnesota, Iowa, and Wisconsin. These mounds, portraying birds, animals, or geometric patterns, were usually used for burials, but they had few funeral offerings.

Far to the south on the Gulf Coast, where Hopewell trade influence had been strong, a variation of the cult continued. Burial mounds here, however, contained figurines and pottery that was quite different from Hopewell relics.

Mound building spread from the Gulf Coast up the Mississippi Valley, and as it spread it changed. The change was largely influenced by Mexico. Huge mounds were built, not for burials but for temples. They had flat tops, serving as platforms for temples or perhaps homes for priests or chieftans. Often these mounds were placed in the Mexican pattern to enclose a plaza. Although mounds were still used for burials in some areas, the burial structures grew smaller with time as more and more effort was put into building the temple mounds.

By 700 A.D. the new cult had spread up the Mississippi Valley as far north as Iowa. In some areas, the new cult, known as the Mississippi Culture, was established among people who were still clinging to the Hopewell traditions. Eventually, however, these people were converted to the new ways.

Large towns were built, and many crops, several of

which originated in Mexico or South America, were cultivated. Artistry for grave offerings also shows strong Mexican influence. Faces and human figures depicted in clay,
stone, and metal probably portrayed gods, including the
long-nosed god that appeared in late Koster relics. Two-
color designs were made on pottery by using a pattern of
wax to shield part of the clay in firing. This "negative"
wax technique developed in Mexico.

By 1000 A.D. the Mississippi Culture was in full
bloom with several large cities up and down the great
valley. Moundville in Alabama was one of these cities, but
it was not the biggest. That honor went to the city in
southern Illinois. It had a population of ten to fifteen
thousand and hundreds of mounds, including the largest
earthen structure ever built by prehistoric man.

Monks Mound, named for trappist monks who lived
on its broad top early in the days of white settlement, was
built in fourteen stages, with the final stage not completed
until about 1100 A.D. Earth was carried to the site in
baskets. The outline of separate basketloads of earth can
still be seen in the sides of a trench dug in the mound.

In addition to building this massive mound, the
Cahokian people, as they are called, also maintained a
walled city that covered more than a hundred acres. The
wall, a stockade of massive logs, was rebuilt three times.

Cahokian life was complex, with distinct social classes
and specialization among the crafts. Trade for grave goods,
matching the trade of the Hopewell cult, extended from
Lake Superior to the Gulf Coast, and eastward to the
shores of the Atlantic. There also may have been regular
trade with Mexico.

Ditches for drainage and irrigation were dug, and salt
was mined from a nearby deposit of brine. Salt and a local
chert were probably important trade commodities.

Although Monks Mound was not used for burial, small mounds nearby were, and one of them covered a remarkable tomb. The man buried was probably a Cahokian king. His body lay on a robe decorated with twelve thousand shell beads. He was surrounded by a rich store of arrowheads, polished stone, and mica, and buried with him were the bodies of six male servants. Nearby, a mass grave contained the bodies of fifty-three women.

The finds suggest that suicide or human sacrifice had become part of the burial ritual. If this was the Cahokian custom, we can again point to Mexican influence.

Like the Hopewell cult before it, the Mississippi Culture declined. Again, we do not know the cause. The decline, however, was gradual and some native Americans may have still been following what were essentially Mississippi traditions in 1540, when Hernando De Soto explored the southeastern territory of North America. De Soto simply reported that the natives had a strong organization that seemed to be flourishing.

More details were provided a few years later by a party of French missionaries who observed the Natchez Indians in Mississippi. The French said the people were divided into two basic classes, the commoners and the nobility. The nobility itself was divided into three ascending levels—honoreds, nobles, and suns. The leader of the tribe was the great sun. The social order was determined by rules of descent through the female side of families.

The French also said that the Natchez practiced human sacrifice and that when a great sun died, his wives and servants were killed and buried with him.

Although the French description may not give a typical picture of the Mississippi Culture, it does seem to explain the mass burial discovered in the shadow of Monks Mound.

Unfortunately, other accounts from explorers gave scant mention of the natives and their traditions, and by the time curiosity about these matters entered the heads of white settlers, the epidemics had taken their terrible toll.

Then only the mounds remained.

Chapter Fourteen

Phantom Visitors

A set of pan pipes found in the Solomon Islands far out in the Western Pacific not only looks like a set of pan pipes made by South American Indians, but also has exactly the same pitch and scale.

In Polynesia, another region of the Pacific, natives have long been growing sweet potatoes, a crop developed by early farmers of the New World.

In Columbus' day, the natives of Central America played a popular game called Patolli. It proved to be Parcheesi, a game invented by the Chinese.

Fragments of five thousand-year-old pottery found on the coast of Ecuador are decorated with the same designs and techniques as pottery of the same age found in Kyushu, the southernmost island of Japan.

Australian aborigines use an atlatl or spear throwing stick, that is identical to atlatls unearthed by archeologists from prehistoric digs on the Great Plains of North America.

Fishermen on the west coast of Africa made unusual use of the remora or sucker fish to catch turtles. A line was

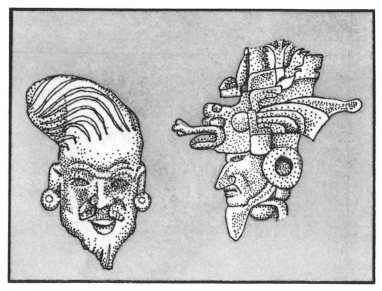

*Carvings of bearded men found in Central America are cited
as support for pre-Columbian visits by Asians or Europeans
to the New World, where natives had little facial hair.*

tied to the fish so that when it attached its suction disk to
the turtle's shell both fish and turtle could be pulled to the
side of the boat. The turtle was hauled aboard and the fish
detached to be used again. When Columbus sailed into the
Caribbean, he found fishermen there using exactly the
same method to catch turtles.

The prehistoric artists of Central America left carvings and figurines of men or gods wearing full beards.
With few exceptions, natives of the New World lack ade-
quate facial hair to grow such beards.

Similarities in mathematics, including the difficult
concept of zero, can be found in early cultures oceans
apart. The same can be said of the craft of metalurgy with
the complex lost wax process for casting delicate figures of
gold and silver having been mastered in both worlds. People of both worlds built pyramids either as temples or
monuments for the dead.

The list can go on and on, but what does it prove? Is
it evidence of unrecorded discovery of the New World
long before Columbus or the Vikings? No. While the simi-

larities are both puzzling and suggestive, we cannot accept them as hard evidence.

By the same token, the differences between Old and New World cultures, which would make even a longer list, do not prove that prehistoric visits from overseas never occurred.

It's a little maddening. All we can say is that there *might* have been prehistoric visits. So the question persists, and unfortunately, the topics is a favorite one among amateur archeologists, who have not been trained to test the facts. With typical enthusiasm for their subject, these amateurs often begin with the premise that visits did occur, and then they set out to marshal information, such as similarities in cultures, that will support their premise.

Professional archeologists, quite correctly, object to this approach to their science. The professionals do have ways to explain how similarities in cultures can and do develop independently.

One explanation rests on an evolutionary process called convergence. It means that environment channels human development and invention. Thus, if a marine environment contains both turtles and remora fish, men will, out of necessity and through experience, eventually discover that the remora can be used to capture turtles. Under the convergence concept, the method evolved independently in both the Caribbean and along the coast of Africa simply because of similar environments.

Convergence undoubtedly played a role in the independent development of the blow gun in the African and Amazon jungles. Both environments contain hollow stemmed plants and other plants that yield poisons. In both regions, game can be stalked under dense cover that allows the hunter to approach within range of a blown dart. So natives, in both these isolated and widely separated regions, invented blow guns that served to stun or killed game with a poison dart.

A second explanation for similarities is based on physical and human limitations. How many ways were there for primitive people to mark a burial? Mounding earth or piling stones over a grave would provide the most permanent monument, and this would lead eventually to pyramid building.

There are really just two ways to increase spearthrusting power. One is to use a pliant shaft, weight it and then release it with a swinging motion, similar to the motion used by an athlete in hammer throw competition. Another more accurate method is to add leverage with a throwing stick or atlatl fitted to the butt of a spear. As the spear is released, the atlatl adds an extra boost, serving, in effect, as an extension of the throwing arm. With the concept of limitations in mind, it is really not too surprising to find spear weights and atlatls in both Old and New World archeological sites.

But even if we accept convergence and limitations as a logical explanation for the long list of similarities, there are some things that remain puzzling. The rules of Parcheesi and Patolli are alike in every detail. It seems almost impossible that the game could have been invented independently. Could latecomers, migrating across the ice of the Bering Strait, have brought the game from Asia to the New World, or was there a long ocean voyage, perhaps several voyages, across the vast Pacific?

There is considerable support, even from some archeologists, for a Pacific crossing. The currents are right for it. A strong flow off the coast of Japan, running as swiftly as twenty-four miles an hour, could carry a ship into the northern Pacific where an eastward current running five to ten miles an hour could carry the ship to the New World.

If the reports of early white explorers in British Columbia are to be believed, it seems probable that currents did carry ships across the Pacific in prehistoric times. The explorers said that Indians along the Canadian coast kept Japanese slaves, presumed to be shipwrecked sailors.

We know of at least one crossing in historic times. It was recorded in 1815, after a storm dismasted a Japanese junk off the coast of Osaka. The boat drifted helplessly for seventeen months until it was spotted off Santa Barbara, California, and towed into port there. Three Japanese fishermen survived the ordeal to tell their story. A junk is a seaworthy boat, and although we think of a bark or dugout canoe in connection with prehistoric men, as long as twenty-six hundred years ago China had boats that could be sailed to the Indian ocean and back. Why not to America as well?

Such a voyage may have been reported in 499 A.D. by a Buddhist missionary. The report was written into the record of the Chinese court in Peking when Hui-Shen, the missionary, appeared before the emperor. Hui-Shen told of a long voyage to the east that he and five other missionaries made in 456 A.D.

He said they reached a land called Fu Sang, where a peaceful people lived in unwalled cities under the rule of royal families. The people knew how to make paper and they had written language. Their clothing was made from the inner bark of trees. The voyage to Fu Sang and back covered seventeen thousand miles, but Hui-Shen concluded that it was a worthy venture because he and his fellow missionaries had great success in converting the people to Buddhism.

Hui-Shen's brief description seems to fit what we know of prehistoric Central America, the only region of the New World where a written language was invented.

No one can really say where Fu Sang was. No traces of Buddhism have been found by New World archeologists. This, however, does not necessarily prove that Fu Sang was not in the New World.

New beliefs or inventions don't pass from one people to another unless there is a need for them. We have already seen how the Piutes of the American plains dealt with the horse, and how the people of Central America invented the wheel but failed to take advantage of it. Another classic example of the resistance to change can be found in Greenland, which was occupied by Viking settlers from 985 to about 1400 A.D. Eskimos were in close contact with the settlers, but the only things the Eskimos retained from this contact were a few words from the Old Norse language and a scattering of metal tools.

What kind of evidence will archeologists require as proof that prehistoric visitors were something more than phantoms? This is hard to answer because archeologists themselves rarely agree on the interpretation of evidence.

There has been one discovery, however, that has come perhaps closer than anything else to the proof archeologists will accept. The discovery, at least, produced tangible evidence.

The key find occurred in the fall of 1956 when Emilio Estrada, an amateur archeologist, was excavating a shell mound in the Province of Guayas on the coast of his native Ecuador. The mound, a refuse heap of early habitation, contained bones of fish and deer, a few stone tools, and fishhooks made of shell. The people who left the mound may have practiced some farming, but they seemed to be basically hunters and gatherers who lived a fairly primitive existence.

Thus, Estrada was startled to come upon heavily eroded fragments of pottery. The fragments looked similar to some of the earliest known pottery from the Peruvian coast that dated back to about 2000 B.C.

Estrada's discovery sparked intense interest in the entire region and it was not long before more discoveries made exciting news. From a site near Valdivia, Ecuador, at a level laid down five thousand years ago, other pottery fragments came to light. At the time they were the oldest known samples of pottery in the New World. Their age, however, was just one cause for excitement.

The fragments came from bowls and vases that had been decorated with care, either by scratching or jabbing marks in the wet clay with a stick or by building up designs by applying ridges of clay. Some designs had even been pressed into the clay with rocker-like stamps.

This was not the kind of advanced technique one would expect to be used on the earliest pottery. In fact, the early pottery of other regions showed evidence of very crude beginnings with little or no attention to design. In addition, there was something about the design on these Ecuadorian fragments that attracted the keen attention of two pottery specialists. The fragments, it seemed, were similar, in many cases identical, to fragments of pottery left by the Jamon culture, which flourished about 3000 B.C. on Kyushu, the southernmost island of Japan.

The specialists, Betty J. Meggers and Clifford Evans, did not draw any sudden conclusions. After studying the samples of pottery from the Ecuador sites, the two went to Japan to make exhaustive comparisons with Jamon samples. When Meggers and Evans returned, however, they were convinced that Jamon sailors, probably fishermen, had been caught by a storm that damaged their ship beyond repair. Then, the currents carried them on a journey of eight thousand miles to the coast of Ecuador.

Not only did the pottery samples match, but the digs

themselves also showed remarkable similarities. With few exceptions, the Jamon refuse mounds could have passed for the mounds that Estrada and others had excavated in Ecuador.

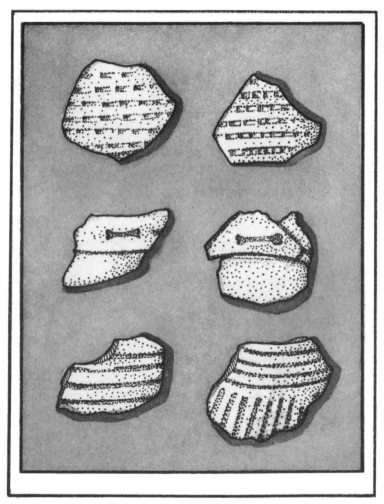

Pottery patterns from Japan, left, show a remarkable similarity to patterns on pottery found in Ecuador, right, and give strong support to early trans-Pacific voyages.

The designs in the pottery of both regions had been made with the same techniques and combination of techniques, and it was possible to trace the evolution of these techniques in Japan only. No evidence in Ecuador gave any indication that the techniques had evolved there.

Meggers and Evans published their conclusions in 1966. Since then, older and cruder pottery has been found in Ecuador and other regions of the New World. While the recent finds have raised some doubt about the conclusions of Meggers and Evans, it is hard just the same to explain the similarities in style and technique through the workings of convergence or limitations. The environment, after all, has little to do with what kind of patterns are put on a clay pot. And while there are limits to designing methods, it is remarkable that Jamon and Ecuadorian potters combined exactly the same methods.

If nothing else, the finds in Ecuador give a strong probability to the question of prehistoric visits. But even archeologists who believe that visits probably occurred will point out that the impact of such visits was minimal.

We have already seen the marked differences in Old and New World farming, one of developing man's most important endeavors. Despite resistance to change, if there had been prehistoric contact it surely would have been reflected in agriculture.

Language experts have searched for parallels in prehistoric tongues of the Old and New Worlds without finding any conclusive proof of contact. True, there are a few scattered cases of similar sounding words, but the general conclusion is that languages evolved independently.

There is another good cause for looking at the cases for prehistoric visits with a skeptical eye. This is the longstanding prejudice against New World natives, the same prejudice that led to the "vanished race" theory on the mound builders. Fortunately, the idea that New World natives could not invent anything on their own without outside help is fast disappearing.

The fact is that natives of North and South America were remarkably resourceful and inventive. We can thank them for the hollow rubber ball, the syringe, the tobacco pipe, the hammock, the parka, the poncho, the snowshoe, and the toboggan sled—all New World inventions. After the discovery of America, the Old World gained more than fifty new foods, all developed by New World farmers. Some historians have suggested that many concepts in the United States Constitution were influenced by American Indians of the eastern seaboard, who had developed a democratic government.

As for the level of civilization attained in the New World we have only to look at the Incan Empire.

Chapter Fifteen

Most Civilized

When the peoples of two empires met in the highlands of the Andes in 1532, swift disaster befell one of the most refined civilizations of the New World. It became a lost civilization.

Even today, after years of digging and research, our knowledge of the Incan Empire remains incomplete, but we know enough to marvel. Ironically, one of the most puzzling marvels is that the Incas, with their long heritage of victory in war and with an army of fifty thousand well-trained men led by veteran generals, fell to a band of a hundred and eighty Spaniards commanded by a bold but illiterate adventurer.

The Incas represented the ultimate growth and mix of South American cultures that began thousands of years ago. In fact, it might be said that the Incas had progressed too far, that they had become too refined to deal with foreign ruffians who were driven by little more than a lust for gold and silver.

From Ecuador to Chile, Incan rulers, the products of royal breeding similar to that of Egyptian pharaohs,

The network of Incan roads stretched from Columbia all the
way south to the border of Bolivia.

governed an empire of three hundred and fifty thousand
square miles. To link this empire, Incan engineers had
built a network of roads that matched the roads of the
Romans. There were also aqueducts and irrigation canals,

large cities and temples, all built without the aid of the wheel.

Incan government was sophisticated. When the Spanish leader, Francisco Pizarro, deceived and captured Atahualpa, the ruler of the Incas, the government, like any good bureaucracy, continued to function. No one but Atahualpa, however, could make the necessary decisions to destroy the invaders. The army would not move without orders. And the orders never came. Then, when the Spanish murdered Atahualpa, the government itself collapsed. The Incan empire fell to ruin.

The Incas had united both the highland cultures of the Andes and the lowland cultures of the coastal valleys, and this mixture of cultures gave the empire remarkable vigor both in its government and its arts. But tracing the story of the Incas and cultures that they combined has not been an easy task for archeologists. Success has come through diverse methods.

Painstaking classification of pottery fragments has made it possible to identify and place in time the many cultures and eras involved. Most Peruvian archeologists are pottery experts. Aerial photography has located the ruins of several "lost cities" that went unnoticed at ground level, and concentrated excavation in isolated valleys has brought to light long chronicles of human occupation.

Even though the Incans originated in the highlands, a review of the record obtained from an excavation in one of the lowland valleys will illustrate the span and variety of Peru's prehistory.

Excavation in the Virú Valley, begun in 1946, by the Institute of Andean Research, revealed that the first human occupation dated back to about 2500 B.C. when coastal fishermen lived in crude pit houses that were roofed with thatch. Though fishing provided a primary food source, these first residents also grew gourds, squash, and beans on small plots. They harvested wild cotton for their textiles and wove baskets, but they had no pottery and still depended on stone as the raw material for their tools.

Pottery appeared in the valley about 1200 B.C. with the dawn of a new era that brought great progress in the arts. Though crude and plain at first, pottery was soon being designed with images of a cat-like god. The cult of the cat or jaguar continued in some regions of Peru for two thousand years.

For the people of the Virú Valley, the greatest gift of the new era was the appearance of corn. This crop improved the living standard substantially and led eventually to the first appearance of villages in the valley. These communities, which date back to about 500 B.C., consisted of twenty to thirty one- or two-room houses made with stone or adobe. The houses were built on the slopes of the valley well above the Virú River. The location suggests to the archeologists that the people had started to irrigate their crops with check dams and canals.

By the year 1 A.D the small towns had given way to much larger communities with buildings made of several joined, rectangular rooms, seemingly added as families grew. These communities spread across the floor of the valley, and at the same time, stone-walled forts were erected on six strategically located hills. Pyramid temples rose inside these citadels, indicating that they served both a religious and military purpose.

The closeness of the communities to the forts would have made it possible for the people to retreat behind the safety of stone walls in time of danger. We don't know exactly what this danger was or where it came from. The attacks may have come across the deserts from neighboring valleys or down from the mountains. Whatever the source, danger apparently increased.

Despite threat of attack, flourishing of culture continued. Soon after the birth of Christ, farmers improved their yields, population expanded, governments strengthened, artistic skill and production bloomed, and medicine developed to a surprising level. In some regions of Peru, doctors were able to graft bone, perform successful amputations, and even practice trepanning, in which the skull was bored to remove a brain tumor. The period of growth and progress at Virú continued for eight centuries.

The valleys' population grew to at least twenty-five thousand. The government ordered construction of four fortified temples, each located on rocky spurs that could be easily defended at the upper end of the valley.

The main government buildings were built around a large brick pyramid that rose eighty feet above the plain at the lower end of the valley. Large apartment houses, honeycombed with rooms that were evidently entered from the roof, provided living quarters that were far from luxurious. Judging from the public works such as fortifications, temples, and irrigation canals, it can be concluded that the government demanded hard labor from its citizens. There was little leisure, and the only luxury people could look forward to was in death. Graves were lavishly provided with elaborately woven cloth, gold ornaments, and a specially fine funeral pottery, much better than ordinary cooking ware.

Although cultures had similar patterns in other valleys, there remained many local variations, showing that the Virú Valley remained relatively isolated for long periods. Just the same, judging from the fortifications, efforts to consolidate the coastal valleys under a single government were being made repeatedly. A successful consolidation, however, did not occur until about 800 A.D. It was accomplished by the Mochica, a warring people who originated in the Moche and Chicama valleys north of Virú. In all, the Mochica empire encompassed six valleys.

Mochica pottery was decorated with realistic scenes, some of which depicted harsh punishment, including facial scarring and amputation. Such scenes have led to the conclusion that the Mochica conquest was a cruel one. But the Mochica were also expert engineers. In the Moche Valley they built two great pyramids, and an aqueduct that remained in use until flood waters destroyed it in 1925. At one spot, the aqueduct spanned a dry gorge on a stone bridge fifty feet high.

During Mochica rule, Virú's old government center was abandoned and a new one begun on a knoll at the southern edge of the valley. Enclosed by a massive adobe wall that ran for eight hundred feet around the knoll, the new center was to have a brick pyramid and government buildings with many rooms. Not far from the construction site was a compound enclosed by rough brick walls, where the labor pool was housed in what appears, to the archeologists, to be concentration camp conditions. The people of Virú apparently did not fare well under Mochica rule, but the rule did not last long.

The new government center was not yet completed when a new wave of conquest swept into the valley. This time it came from the highlands of Bolivia. By about 1000 A.D., these highlanders had conquered the entire Peruvian coast.

The conquest brought with it a new style of black, molded pottery and a new architecture. The highlanders, called Tiahuanaco, directed the construction of large rectangular compounds near the mouth of the Virú River. Enclosing an orderly arrangement of rooms, some of these compounds measured four hundred by seven hundred and fifty feet.

Irrigation continued and the valley's population remained stable under what seems to have been an easier rule than before. There was, however, a continuing demand for a large labor force for public works. The greatest undertaking by far, under Tiahuanaco rule, was the construction of roads across the deserts. These roads, which linked the valleys and thus united the Tiahuanaco conquest, were thirty feet wide and lined on both sides with adobe walls that kept back the drifting sand. The roads were so well engineered and built that they were incorporated with little change into the Incan highway system some five hundred years later.

The Tiahunanaco rule collapsed about 1300 A.D., giving way to the Chimú Empire, which continued to hold the coastal valleys under one government. The Chimú people came from the Moche Valley, immediately north of Virú. It was in the Moche Valley that the Chimú built Chan Chan, their capital city.

Chan Chan flourished to become the center of the arts as well as the government. The Chimú excelled particularly in weaving and dying. Their textiles were among the finest ever produced by prehistoric craftsmen. Colorful feathers were often woven into the cloth to make garments and wall hangings of outstanding brilliance. Some of the feathers were imported from tropical jungles on the far side of the high Andes. Woodcarving and metalwork with copper, gold, and silver were also raised to high arts, and molded pottery was of such good quality that it could serve either for daily use or for grave offerings.

But while Chan Chan prospered, the Virú Valley suffered. Under Chimú rule, Virú population declined, and irrigated land shrank to the upper end of the valley.

Thus, in 1470 A.D., when the Incan soldiers arrived, they found a people whose greatness had passed.

While the people of the valleys had a heritage of isolation combined with the need for irrigation, which required, in turn, a strong central government, the highlands where the Incas began had a different heritage.

Even in the days of hunting and fishing, highland tribes were not isolated. They knew their neighboring tribes and quickly learned both the arts of diplomacy and warfare.

When agriculture began in the high plateaus of the Andes between four and five thousand years ago, it took a different form from the crop-based agriculture of the valleys. Instead of raising beans and squash and other crops, the first highland farmers were herders. They domesticated the vicuña, alpaca, and llama, all of which yielded both wool and meat. Rainfall in the highlands provided ample grazing land for these early ranchers.

The herding life encouraged independence. No central authority was needed to build irrigation dams and canals. Even when highlanders began cultivating crops, there was little need for irrigation because of the frequent mountain rainstorms. Early crops were the potato and coca. Potatoes were preserved through alternate drying and freezing to produce a food called chuno. Coca leaves were chewed as a stimulant, a practice that survives in the Andes to this day.

One theory holds that corn originated in the highlands of the Andes, but if this is true it is hard to explain why it did not become an important crop there until about 1000 B.C., well after Mexican farmers began cultivating corn. In any case, the advent of corn quickened the pace of life in the highlands. Construction of pyramid temples began, and weaving and metal work improved.

When scarce flatland was fully cultivated, Incan farmers terraced the steep hillsides to expand their acreage.

In about 500 B.C., fortifications and walls around hilltop pyramids began to be built. The walls probably served both for defense and for penning livestock. At about this time, highland farmers discovered that some plants could be propagated from cuttings as well as from seed, and this discovery, combined with a growing dependence on corn, increased the demand for tillable land. In the steep highlands, additional land could be obtained only by terracing. Some terraces were built along such steep slopes that the cultivation strips were no more than two or three feet wide. Dung from domestic animals was used to replenish the nutrients in the terrace soils.

Building of walls, fortifications, pyramids, and the terraces required forces of workers organized under central control. Thus, centralized government came at last to the highlands, but since it came later there than it did in the valleys, the highlanders retained their spirit of independence.

From about year one to 500 A.D., the arts flourished, with each region or tribal unit developing distinct styles in weaving, pottery, and other crafts. Today's experts have no trouble identifying various tribes from the pottery of this era. Study of the stars and planets reached such a high level among the Nazca people of the high plateaus in southern Peru that they were able to establish a calendar that was almost as accurate as the Mayan calendar.

Huge patterns carved across acres and acres of open plain probably served to aid Nazca astronomers in their observations, but the patterns may have had some other purpose that has not yet been discovered. The Nazcas were famous for their tapestry, and the patterns on the plain may have simply been prompted by the creative urge, expressed on a grand scale.

The first five centuries after Christ were also marked by increased contact with neighboring tribes and expansion of trade. Trade apparently extended down to the coastal valleys, because the potato was introduced there, and later coastal farmers began the highland practice of raising animals for wool and meat. In about 500 A.D., unification of tribes under centralized control increased in the highlands. The movement made it possible for the Tiahuanaco eventually to mount a successful conquest of the coastal valleys.

Although much of Peru came under Tiahuanaco rule in about 1000 A.D., there were regions of the highlands that remained independent. One of these regions bordered Lake Titicaca in southern Peru. This was Inca territory.

Although famous as fierce fighters, the Incas were not cruel. They ruled wisely and learned to adopt the best features of the governments and the cultures that they conquered. As a consequence, some of their neighbors, those who suffered under harsh rule, welcomed Incan conquest.

Early in their origins, the Incas established a royal family, which gave their government stability. Further stability rose from the organization of their army. The young men drafted and trained for the army were not idle during times of peace. Instead they built roads, temples, walls, and fortifications.

With stability and wise rule, the Incan empire spread northward along the highlands. According to legend, their capital city of Cusco was established in about 1200 A.D. It stood on a plateau ten thousand feet above sea level.

The city became a cultural as well as an economic and political center. All roads led to Cusco. The main road, which eventually stretched two thousand miles across both Peru and Ecuador, did not wind and twist like typical mountain roads. It followed as straight a path as possible. If a ridge was in the path, Incan engineers simply carved steps up one side of the ridge and down the other. Deep gorges were spanned with suspension bridges, with twisted plant fibers serving as the bridge cables.

Most sections of the road were fifteen feet wide, and in heavily traveled areas, the road was paved with stones. These paving stones were joined so well that even today it is impossible to slide a knife blade into the cracks between them.

Incan expansion continued until all but a few fierce tribes to the north and the Chimú Empire of the coastal valleys remained outside the Incan sphere. The Chimú military leaders believed that the northern tribes would prevent Incan attack from the north. For this reason, the Chimú defenses were built along the southern borders only. This was a crucial mistake. Always good diplomats, the Incan leaders subdued and then made peace with the northern tribes, enlisting their help in attacking Chimú from the north.

The coastal conquest was thus achieved without serious losses to the Incas. As before, many regions of the Chimú empire welcomed the conquest. The Incans, al-

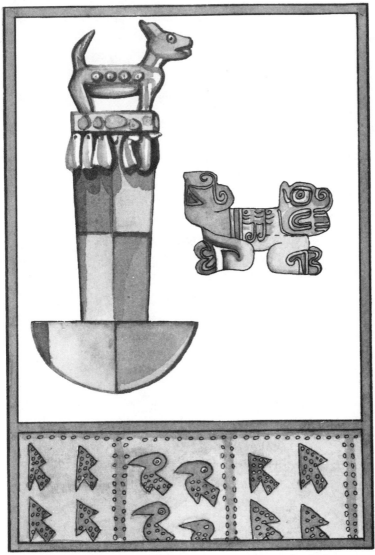

Delicate craftsmanship of Peruvian gold workers include a ceremonial knife (left), a jaguar (right), and a hammered band decorated with a bird motif.

ready influenced by the Chimú culture, preserved many of its traditions. In addition, Incan government, both stable and liberal, brought new security and new freedoms to the people.

With the land united and at peace, Incan engineers incorporated the eight-hundred-mile coastal road into their highway system by building several secondary roads linking the coast route with the highland route.

Llama caravans carried trade goods throughout the realm. Swift runners brought messages to and from Cusco. It took just five days for a message, carried in relays, to travel from Quito in Ecuador to the Incan capital, a distance of fifteen hundred miles. Special shelters were built along the route for the runners. There were other shelters for the pack trains, where traders could find food and rest as well as fodder for their animals.

Ironically, the roads gave Pizarro and his men easy access to the heartland of the Inca Empire. Saying they came in peace, the Spaniards were not just unopposed but were actually guided toward Cusco. Pizarro's march was slowed temporarily when his horses lost their iron shoes through hard wear on the paved route. This problem was solved when new shoes were forged, not of iron, but of silver.

The abundant gold and silver in the land of the Incas was what the Spaniards sought, and they were able to amass a great store of treasure after they captured Atahualpa and held him for ransom. The Incans saw no monetary value in gold and silver. They simply treasured the metals for their beauty and the things it was possible to make with them.

Tragically, all the plates, cups, jewels, shields, headdresses, knives, figurines, and other beautifully worked artifacts that the Incans gave to free their leader were melted down into gold and silver bars by the Spaniards. Then, instead of realeasing their hostage as promised, the Spaniards murdered him.

Thus, did the civilizations of two worlds meet.

B I B L I O G R A P H Y

BYERS, DOUGLAS S., editor, *The Prehistory of the Tehuacán Valley,* Austin, University of Texas Press, 1967.

CERAM, C. W., *The First Americans: A Story of North American Archeology,* New York, Harcourt Brace Jovanovich, 1971.

COE, MICHAEL D., *America's First Civilization: Discovering the Olmec,* New York, American Heritage, 1968.

COLLIER, JOHN, *Indians of the Americas,* New York, New American Library of World Literature, 1963.

DEUEL, LEO, *Conquistadors without Swords, Archaeologists in the Americas,* New York, Schocken Books, 1974.

DÍAZ DEL CASTILLO, BERNAL, *The Discovery and Conquest of Mexico, 1519–21,* New York, Farrar, Straus, 1956.

DRAGOO, D. W., *Mounds for the Dead,* Pittsburgh, Carnegie Museum, 1963.

FARB, PETER, *Man's Rise to Civilization, the Cultural Ascent of the Indians of North America,* New York, Bantam, 1978.

———, *Humankind,* Boston, Houghton Mifflin, 1978.

FITTING, J. E., editor, *The Development of North American Archeology,* Garden City, N.Y., Doubleday & Co., 1973.

FREUCHEN, PETER, *Book of the Eskimo,* Cleveland, World Publishing Co., 1961.

GIDDINGS, J. L., *Ancient Men of the Arctic,* New York, Alfred A. Knopf, Inc., 1967.

HARRIS, MICHAEL, *Cannibals and Kings, The Origins of Cultures,* New York, Random House, 1977.

HAURY, E. W., *The Hohokam: Desert Farmers and Craftsmen,* Tucson, University of Arizona Press, 1976.

HELM, JUNE, editor, *Pioneers of American Anthropology,* Seattle, University of Washington Press, 1966.

HIBBEN, FRANK C., *Treasure in the Dust,* New York, J. P. Lippincott Co., 1951.

———, *Digging Up America,* New York, Hill and Wang, 1960.

HOPKINS, D. M., *The Beringia Land Bridge,* Stanford, CA, Stanford University Press, 1967.

JENNINGS, J. D., *Prehistory of North America,* New York, Mc-Graw-Hill, 1974.

KROEBER, THEODORA, *Ishi,* Berkeley, University of California Press, 1961.

——— and HEIZER, ROBERT F., *Almost Ancestors, the First Californians,* San Francisco, Sierra Club, 1968.

LEAKEY, L. S. B., *et al, Pleistocene Man at Calico,* San Bernardino, CA., County Museum Association, 1972.

MACGOWAN, KENNETH, and HESTER, JOSEPH A., JR., *Early Man in the New World,* Garden City, N.Y., Doubleday & Co., 1962.

McHARGUE, GEORGESS and ROBERTS, MICHAEL, *A Field Guide to Conservation Archeology in North America,* New York, J. P. Lippincott Co., 1977.

MARTIN, P. S. AND WRIGHT, H. F., editors, *Pleistocene Extinctions: Search for a Cause,* New Haven, Conn., Yale University Press, 1967.

MEGGERS, B. J., *Prehistoric America,* Chicago, Aldine-Atherton, 1972.

OSWALT, W. H., *This Land Was Theirs,* New York, John Wiley and Sons, 1973.

PATTERSON, T. C., *America's Past,* Glenwood, Ill., Scott, Foresman, 1973.

RILEY, C. L., *et al,* editors, *Man Across the Sea,* Austin, University of Texas Press, 1971.

SANDERS, WILLIAM T. and MARINO, JOSEPH, *New World Prehistory, Archeology of the American Indian*, Englewood Cliffs, N.J., Prentice-Hall, 1970.

SILVERBERG, ROBERT, *Mammoths, Mastadons and Man*, New York, McGraw-Hill, 1970.

SNOW, DEAN, *The Archeology of North America*, New York, Viking Press, 1976.

SPENCER, R. F. and JENNINGS, J. D. *et al*, *The Native Americans*, New York, Harper and Row, 1977.

TRENTO, SALVATORE M., *The Search for Lost America, the Mystery of the Stone Ruins*, Chicago, Contemporary Books, 1978.

VON HAGEN, VICTOR W., *The Aztec, Man and Tribe*, New York, New American Library, 1958.

————, *The World of the Maya*, New York, New American Library, 1960.

WEAVER, M. P., *The Aztecs, Maya, and Their Predecessors*, New York, Seminar Press, 1972.

WEDEL, WALDO R., *Prehistoric Man on the Great Plains*, Norman, University of Oklahoma Press, 1961.

WILLEY, GORDON R. and SABLOFF, JEREMY A., *History of American Archeology*, San Francisco, W. H. Freeman, 1974.

ZUBROW, EZRA B. W., FRITZ, MARGARET C., and FRITZ, JOHN M., editors, *New World Archeology* (reprint of articles from *Scientific American*), San Francisco, W. H. Freeman, 1974.

INDEX

Abejas culture, 117
Abrigo do Sol (Brazil), pottery making, 57–63
Adena mound cult, 137–140
Adovasio, James M., Meadowcroft research, 66–67, 68, 71
agriculture: Incan, 165–166; Koster, 99–110; plant domestication, Tehuacán, 111–119; spread to North America, 136–137; Teotihuacán, 123, 126, 129; Virú, 161
Ajalpán phase of Tehuacán culture, 117
Ajuerado phase of Tehuacán culture, 116
Akmak culture, stone tools, 39–40
Alaska: land link with Siberia theories, 14–17; southern migration from, 18–19
alpaca, domestication, 165
Amazon Indians, Wasúsus and pottery making of Abrigo do Sol, 54–63
amino acid dating, 22–26
Anderson, Douglas D., Alaskan relic finds, 39–41, 52
Andean cultures, 158–170
animal domestication: Koster, 104; Tehuacán, 117, 119; Incan, 165; in New World, 118–119
animal effigies: Koster, 109; Red Paint People, 93–94

animals, extinction of Pleistocene, 73–86
Archaic Indians, Red Paint People, 88–96
Archaic tool tradition, 41
archeology: and derivation of native Americans, 15; early finds, 3–12
Arctic region, stone tool culture, 33–43, 52
Arctic Small Tool Tradition at Onion Portage, 41
Arizona, Hohokam culture, 130
army, Incan, 167–168
arrow points, Koster, 109
art: Andean, 166; Folsom spear points as, 79–80; Hopewell, 140–142; Koster, 106–108
arthritis, in skeletons of Red Paint People, 92
Asia, land link migration route theory, 13–21
aspartic acid, in amino acid racemization, 24, 25
astronomy, Nazca, 167
Atahualpa, Incan ruler, 160, 170
atlatl, 148, 151
auk, 93
Aztecs, 120, 125; conquest of Mexico, 131

Bada, Jeffry L., 22
bands: hunters, 80; Wasúsus, 54–63

bark, Meadowcroft finds, 69
baskets: Koster, 104, 106; Meadowcroft 68, 69
Bat Cave, Mexico, 113
bean seeds, Meadowcroft finds,
68
beekeeping, 119
Bell, Robert E., El Inga finds,
44–49
Berger, Rainer, 9, 10
Beringia, land link, 13–21
Bering Straits, land link, 15
biface disks, Arctic tool finds,
39
biface knives, Arctic tools, 39
blades, Red Paint People, 92–
93
Bird, Junius B., 15, 45
bison, extinction, 74, 81
blades, see stone tools
boat theory, migration, 14–15
Bolivia, Andean cultures, 159,
163
bone (s) : amino acid dating,
22–26; charred, 11, 12; Clovis
weapons, 83–94; Meadow-
croft, 67, 69; Red Paint
People, 89–92
Bonnichsen, Robson, 83
bow and arrow: Koster, 109;
Wasúsus, 56
Brazil, Abrigo do Sol, 54–63
Brown, James A., 101
bureaucracy, Incan, 160
burial mounds, 144; Adena,
137–139; Cahokian, 146;
Hopewell, 140
burial sites: Clovis, 82; Koster,
104–105; Red Paint People,
87–96; Tehuacán, 116
burials, Virú, 162
burins: Arctic, 40–41; El Inga,
47, 48, 49

Cahokian people, 145–146
calendar, Nazca, 167

Calico Hills, hearth, 3–12, 21
Calico International Conference, 10
California, bone dating, 23–25
camel, extinction, 15, 75, 81
Campus site (Alaska), tool
finds, 35
canals, Teotihuacán, 121
canoes: Koster, 104; Red Paint
People, 92
Cape Denbigh, Arctic tool
finds, 37, 42
Cape Krusenstern, Arctic tool
finds, 37
carbon 14 dating, 20–21; of
Abrigo do Sol charcoal, 62;
of Clovis artifacts, 81; corncobs, 114; Meadowcroft, 68,
69; Red Paint People artifacts, 91; see also dating
caribou: bone tools, 21; hunting of, 34
caves, Tehuacán excavation,
114
Central America, Teotihuacán
city-state, 120–131
centralization, Teotihuacán,
127
Chan Chan, Tiahuanaco, capital city, 164
change, resistance to, 52–53,
153, 156
charcoal: dating, Abrigo do Sol,
62; finds, 11, 12; from Meadowcroft, 67
chert trade, mound culture,
142, 145
Chile, Andean cultures, 158
Chimú Empire, 164; Inca conquest of, 168–169
China, and pre-Columbian
New World, 152–153
chinampas water farming, 123
choppers: Arctic tool industry,
39, 41; pebble tool culture, 11
Choris culture, 42

Church of Jesus Christ of Latter-Day Saints, 14
Citadel (Teotihuacán), 125
cities: Incan, 168; Mississippi
culture, 145
city-state, Teotihuacán, 120–
131
class distinctions: Adena cult,
137–138; Cahokian, 145; Ho-
koham, 130
Clements, Thomas, 6
climate: Ice Age, 17–18, 75–76;
Meadowcroft Rockshelter,
70; Teotihuacán culture, 129
Clovis, New Mexico, finds, 77–
85
Clovis hunters, use of red pigment, 88–89
Cobleskill, New York, tool
find, 11, 21
coca, Incan cultivation, 165
Colombia, Andean cultures,
159
Columbus, Christopher, 149
combs, Red Paint People, 93,
94
convergence, and cultural similarities, 150–151
cooking: clay balls for, 135,
136; Koster, 106
copper: Adena, 139; Hopewell,
140–142; Koster, 108; Red
Paint People, 88
core-blade tool industry, El
Inga, 47–48
corn: Andean, 161, 165; Tehuacán, 111–119
Cortez, Hernando, 120, 122,
131
Coxcatlán phase of Tehuacán
culture, 116–117
crafts, Teotihuacán, 121
Cro-Magnon man, 26
Cusco, Incan capital, 168, 170

daggers, Red Paint People, 93
dating: amino acid, 22–26; tree
ring, 34; see also carbon 14
dating
Del Mar, California, bone
find, 23
De Soto, Hernando, 146
diseases, brought by explorers,
133
dogs: 104, 105; Red Paint People, 92; Tehuacán, 117, 119
Dick, Herbert, 113
drainage systems, 105, 121, 145
Dry Creek, Arctic relics, 43

Ecuador: Andean cultures, 158,
168, 170; El Inga tool finds,
44; and pre-Columbian visits
to New World, 153–156
effigies, 93–94, 109, 136
effigy mounds, 143
elephant, extinction, 15, 74,
75, 78
El Inga stone tools, 44–53
El Riego phase of Tehuacán
culture, 116
Eskimos: arrival from Asia, 14;
and Arctic tool finds, 33, 34,
35, 36, 42; resistance to
change, 153
Estrada, Emilio, 153–154
extinction, animals, 15–16, 73–
86
Evans, Clifford, 154

farming, New World, 115–119
Fell's Cave (South America),
14–15, 45; tool style, 49
fertility symbols, Abrigo do
Sol, 61–62
figurine cult, Tehuacán, 117
figurines: Hohokam, 130;
Hopewell, 142; at Poverty
Point mounds, 136
fishing: Koster, 106; Red Paint
People, 93

flaked tools, 41
flakes: Arctic microblades, 35;
    pebble tool culture, 11
Floating Gardens of Zochi-
    milco, 123
flutes, Wasúsus, 56
fluting: Clovis spear points, 77;
    El Inga styles, 45; Folsom
    spear points, 79–80
Folsom, New Mexico, kill site
    finds, 79–81
food: Koster, 104, 106, Meadow-
    croft, 67, 69–70; gathering,
    and extinction of animals, 85
Foundation for Illinois Arche-
    ology, 101
France, tools, vs. El Inga tools,
    49
Fu Sang, 152–153
fortifications, Andean, 166

geology: and dating, Calico
    hearth, 10; Ice Age and mi-
    gration route theories, 16–19
Giddings, J. Louis, Jr., 33–39
gift-giving, Adena cult, 139–
    140
gods, Quetzalcoatl, 125
gold, in Andean cultures, 169,
    170
gorgets, 139
government: Incan, 160, 167–
    168; Teotihuacán, 127–129;
    Virú, 162
Graffham, A. Allen, 44–46
grave offerings: Adena, 139;
    Hopewell, 140–142; Koster,
    104, 108; Red Paint People,
    93–95
Great Compound, Teotihua-
    cán, 125
guilds, Teotihuacán, 128
Gunn, Joel, 70–71

hand axes, Calico Hills, 4
harpoon, toggle, 93

hearths, Calico Hills, 3–12
Hohokam culture, 130
Homo sapiens neanderthalen-
    sis, 26–27
Homo sapiens sapiens, 26
Hopewell mound cult, 140–144
horses: in Indian cultures, 52–
    53; extinction, 15, 74–75, 81
houses: Koster, 102, 104, 105;
    Teotihuacán, 127; Viru, 161,
    162
Hui-Shen, 152
human sacrifice, in mound cul-
    tures, 146
hunting: Clovis, 77–78, 81; and
    extinction of Pleistocene
    animals, 81–86; Folsom, 79–
    80; Koster, 109; Meadow-
    croft, 65–72; Tehuacán, 115–
    116

Ice Age: and Arctic tools, 37,
    41; and Beringia, 16–18
Illinois River Valley, Koster ex-
    cavation, 99–100
Incan Empire, 158–170
Indians: Abrigo do Sol pottery,
    54–63; Archaic, Red Paint
    People, 87–96; Arctic tools,
    38, 42; migration theory, 13–
    21; mound cultures, 132–147
Institute of Andean Research,
    160
irrigation: Andean, 165; Caho-
    kian, 145; Hohokam, 130;
    Tiahuanaco, 164; Virú, 161

Jamon culture of Japan, sim-
    ilarities with New World
    cultures, 154–156
Japan, and pre-Columbian
    New World, 152, 154–156
Julius II, Pope, 13
junks, 152

kill sites, 11, 74, 76, 78, 79
knives, Arctic tool industry,
    39–40
Kobuk culture, stone tools, 33,
    37, 40–41
Koster, Theodore, 99, 100
Koster Site, 99-100

Lahren, Larry, 83
Lake Manix, Calico hearth
    discovery, 4–5, 73
language: Old World vs. New
    World, 156; written, 152
La Perra Cave, Mexico, 113
leadership, in hunting bands,
    80
Leakey, Louis S. B., 5–6
Lewisville, Texas, archeologi-
    cal find, 10–11, 21
limitations, and cultural simi-
    larities, 151
llama, domestication, 165

MacNeish, Richard S., 11, 113,
    114, 118
mammoth extinction, 74, 76,
    78, 81
marsh elder, Koster cultivation
    of, 108
Martin, Paul S., 185
mastodon, extinction, 74, 81
Mayan culture, 120–131
Mayer-Oakes, William J., 44–
    49
McMillan, R. Bruce, 101
Meadowcroft Rockshelter,
    Pennsylvania, 64–72
medicine, Viru, 162
Meggers, Betty J., 154
Mengelsdorf, Paul C., 112–113,
    114, 115
metal work: Chimú, 164; In-
    can, 169–170
meteors, iron from, 142
Mexico: and mound cultures,
    136–137, 144, 145, 146; Te-

huacán corn cultivation, 111–
    119; Teotihuacán city-state,
    121–131
mica, 142
microblades, Arctic tool indus-
    try, 35–43
migration: land link theory,
    13–21; motivation for, 27–
    30; and tool traditions, 52
Miller, Albert, 65
Miller, Enrico, 58, 61, 62
Millon, René, 126
Mississippi culture, 144–146
Mixtecs, 118
Moche Valley, 163
Mochica people, 163
Mojave Desert, Calico hearth, 3
Monks Mound, 132–133, 145,
    146
Monte Alban, abandonment of,
    129
mounds, 132–147; Tehuacán,
    117
Moundville, Alabama, 145
Mount Alban people, 117

Nambicauras, and Abrigo do
    Sol, 54–63
Natchez Indians, 146
National Geographic Society,
    6, 58
National Science Foundation,
    114
Nazca people, 167
Neanderthal man, 26–27, 28
Newfoundland, Red Paint Peo-
    ple, 87–96

obsidian: El Inga, 46–47, 49;
    Hopewell, 140; Teotihuacán,
    122
oceans, and Ice Age, 16–17
Old Copper Culture, burials,
    132, 134
Old Copper People, 21, 43, 108

Olmecs, 117, 122; and mound
cultures, 136–137
Onion Porage, tool finds, 34–
43
ornaments, Red Paint People,
93–95

Pacific Ocean: pre-Columbian
crossings, 151–156; Ice Age,
18
Paleolithic culture, 44–53
Palo Blanco phase of Tehuacán culture, 117–118
Parcheesi, 148, 151
Patolli, 148, 151
pebble tool culture, 11–12
Perrón phase of Tehuacán culture, 117
Peru, Andean cultures, 160–170
pipes: Adena, 139; Hopewell,
142
Piute Indians, and horses, 53
Pizarro, Francisco, 160, 170
Plains Indians, and horses, 53–
54
plazas, Teotihuacán, 124–125
Pleistocene epoch, 18; extinction of animals, 75–86
population: and disease, 133;
and extinction of animals,
85; Koster, 108–109; Mississippi culture cities, 145; Tehuacán, 117; of Teotihua-
cán, 126, 128, 129; Virú, 162
Port au Choix (Newfound-
land), Red Paint People,
87–96
potatoes, 165, 167
pottery: Abrigo do Sol, 57–63;
Adena, 139; Ecuadorean,
153–156; Hopewell, 142; Incan, 160; Koster, 100, 109;
Mochica, 163; Tehuacán,
117; Tiahuanaco, 163; Teotihuacán, 129; Virú, 161

Poverty Point, Louisiana,
mound culture, 134–137
Pyramid of the Moon, 121, 124
Pyramid of the Sun, 120, 121,
123–125
pyramids: Hohokam, 130; Teotihuacán, 120, 121, 123–125;
Virú, 161

Quetzalcoatl (god), 125
Quito, Ecuador, tool finds, 44,
45, 46

racemization process, 24, 25
Rainey, Froelich G., 39
red, use by Archaic Indians, 88
red ocher: Adena, 138; Koster,
104; Red Paint People, 95
Red Paint People, 87–96; burials, 132, 134
religion: Clovis hunters, 82–83;
Neanderthals, 27; Red Paint
People, 88–89, 95; Tehuacán,
117; Teotihuacán, 123–125;
Wasúsus, 56
Ritter, Rosemary, 3, 7–9, 10
roads, Incan, 159, 168, 169–170
Rockefeller Foundation, 114
rocks, see stone tools
rock shelters: Abrigo do Sol,
57; Meadowcroft, 64–72
Rogers, M. J., 23
royal family, Incan, 167
runners, as Incan message car-
riers, 170

sacred circles, 137, 140
salt, Cahokian trade, 145
Santa Maria phase of Tehua-
cán culture, 117
Santa Rosa Island, California,
11, 21, 74
Sayles, Ritner, 4, 5
Scandia hunters, 81
Schroeder, Roy A., 22, 25

scrapers: Arctic tool industry,
21, 39–41; Calico Hills, 4;
pebble tool culture, 11
sea levels, Ice Age, 16–17
seeds: Koster, 108; Meadowcroft, 67, 68, 69–70
Serpent Mound, 143
shellfish, Meadowcroft, 67, 70,
72
Siberia: and land bridge, 14–
17; and Arctic tool culture,
43
silver: Hopewell, 142; Incan,
170
Simpson, Ruth Dee, 4, 5, 6, 9
skeletons, Red Paint People,
89–92
Smith, Gerald A., 4, 5, 6
smoking, Adena, 139
soldiers, Teotihuacán 128
Spanish conquest, 120, 121, 131,
158, 160, 170
spear points, Clovis, 77–79; Folsom, 79–80; pebble tool culture, 11–12; Red Paint
People, 92, 94
specialization, Teotihuacán,
128
Stone Age: Abrigo do Sol pottery making, 54–63; El Inga
tool styles, 44–53; extinction
of Pleistocene animals, 73–
86; Meadowcroft Rockshel-
ter, 64–72; Red Paint People,
87–96
stone tools: Abrigo do Sol, 61;
Arctic, 33–43; early finds,
3–12; El Inga, 44–53; Koster,
104; Meadowcroft, 67, 69; at
Onion Portage, 35–43; Red
Paint People, 92
stratification of soil, 34–35
Street of the Dead (Teotihuacán), 121, 123–125, 126
Struever, Stuart, 101, 104
suicide, in mound cultures, 146

sunbursts, Abrigo do Sol pottery, 57, 60, 61–62
sun worshipping: and eastward
migration, 28–29; and
mounds, 136

tablets, Adena grave offerings,
139
tapestry, Nazca, 167
teeth, Red Paint People skeleton, 92
Tehuacán Valley, Mexico, corn
cultivation, 114–119
temples: Teotihuacán, 120,
121, 125, 129; Virú, 161
teosinte, 112–113
Teotihuacán, city-state, 120–
131
Tertiary Period, 16
textiles, Chimú, 164
Tiahuanaco culture, 163–164,
167
Tikal, Mayan city, 128
tobacco, Adena smokers, 139
Toltec empire, 131
tools: Koster, 106; of Red Paint
People, 92; see also stone
tools
totems, Red Paint People, 95
trade: Adena, 139; Andean,
167; Cahokian, 145; Hope-
well, 142–144; Tehuacán,
117, 118; and Teotihuacán
growth, 122
tree ring dating, 34
tripsacum, 112–113
Tuck, James A., 89, 92–93, 95
turkey, domesticated, 118

urban renewal, Teotihuacán,
127, 128

vegetation, Meadowcroft, 70
Venta Salada phase of Tehuacán culture, 118

vicuña, domestication, 165
villages, Virú, 161
Virú, cultures, 160–164
von Puttkamer, W. Jesco, 55–
57, 62

wall carvings, Abrigo do Sol,
57, 60, 61
warfare, and agriculture, 109
Wasúsus, Abrigo do Sol pottery,
54–63
water, Teotihuacán, 123
weapons: of Clovis and Folsom
hunters, 77–84; of Red Paint
People, 92–93

weaving: Chimú, 164; Hopewell, 142; mound cultures,
139
whale effigies, 93–94
wheel, and Indian resistance to
change, 52–53
Wilsall, Montana, Clovis burial
site, 82
women: Stone Age, 71; Wa-
súsus, 56, 61–62
wood work: Koster, 104, 106;
Red Paint People, 92
worship mounds, 137

Yukon, Arctic tool sites, 21, 43